ESG Rating Agencies and Financial Regulation

Dedication

While it is not my usual way with my monographs to make such a defined dedication section, I would like to dedicate this book to two people in particular.

The first person I would like to dedicate this book to is the late Professor Paul Watchman – the 'Godfather' of ESG, as he is known. The world lost Paul on 2 July 2023, and I thought it appropriate to dedicate this book to him. I was fortunate enough to have known Paul personally and had discussed the idea for this book and associated works with him. Given that he led the team that wrote the 'Freshfields Report', which the book relies upon, I was more than aware of my fortune of being able to speak with Paul as a leader in our field, my mentor, and a friend. His insights into what ESG is, and where the field is going, are something I came to rely upon and it felt natural to have his insights, whether personally or through his public-facing works. As I was deep into the writing phase of the book, it came as a tremendous shock to learn that he had tragically passed on, when we were all expecting him to make a full recovery. His loss has caused me to reflect on my relationship with him, his relationship with his field, ESG as a concept and a movement, and how a person should be. I would not attest to whether he was an angel every day of his life because, as I am sure, none of us are, but, to me, he was kind when he had no reason to be, facilitative beyond compare, and most of all just an open book that was substantial in nature. I think the measure of the man is that while I knew I was not the only one fortunate to have him be who he was for me, the incredible stories I have heard and read since his passing of what he meant to other people confirms for me who he was. I, and many others, shall miss him greatly.

My other dedication goes to my new fiancée who, as ever, must suffer living with somebody writing multiple books in such a short space of time. Her patience and understanding are virtues I could only wish for.

ESG Rating Agencies and Financial Regulation

A Signalling Theory Approach

Daniel Cash

Reader in Law, Aston Law School, Aston University, UK

Edward Elgar
PUBLISHING

Cheltenham, UK • Northampton, MA, USA

Published by
Edward Elgar Publishing Limited
The Lypiatts
15 Lansdown Road
Cheltenham
Glos GL50 2JA
UK

Edward Elgar Publishing, Inc.
William Pratt House
9 Dewey Court
Northampton
Massachusetts 01060
USA

A catalogue record for this book
is available from the British Library

Library of Congress Control Number: 2023951410

This book is available electronically in the **Elgar**online
Law subject collection
http://dx.doi.org/10.4337/9781035315055

ISBN 978 1 0353 1504 8 (cased)
ISBN 978 1 0353 1505 5 (eBook)

Printed and bound by CPI Group (UK) Ltd, Croydon, CR0 4YY

Contents

Foreword

I have no compunction in saying that my young and vibrant Geneva-based United Nations Environment Programme Finance Initiative (UNEP FI) team of the early 2000s was renegade, off reservation, and worked on the unusual UN basis of asking for 'forgiveness not permission'. In short, we flew below the radar of the normal UN system and that's why we got things done, ultimately and unimaginably, given our wafer-thin resources, to influence the financial system and the, for now, all-powerful institutions which populate it.

Amongst other work, we created ESG in 2004, commissioned the 2005 Freshfields Report challenging the investment status quo, delivered the UN Principles for Responsible Investment (UNPRI) in 2006, and trained thousands of bankers in what would become ESG. Essentially, as a guerrilla operation, we pulled off a 'sleight of hand' that still resonates in the global financial system today.

Is ESG perfect? Absolutely not. Is ESG equivalent to sustainability? Absolutely not. Is the UNPRI a magic game-changer? Absolutely not.

Collectively, however, these developments create a powerful signal to the investment chain from end beneficiaries (the pensioners depending on asset owners) through to investee corporations across public and private markets and all the complex intermediaries in between.

The signal?

The nature of risk is changing, metastasising, morphing, converging in a manner that undermines the investment world's previous risk calculations and opens investment and commercial opportunities through the new markets needed to address critically needed change in the global political economy. Why are the large, mainstream credit rating agencies (CRAs), as well as the growing band of nascent specialist CRAs, finding ESG so challenging? A view from the edge of space: we are in the eye of the gathering storm – striving to transition from 250 years of extractive capitalism to a, as yet, elusive regenerative model. There should be no surprise that a critical signalling function provided by CRAs, deeply embedded in present-day globalised, financialised, seemingly, seamless markets is so challenging with great change gathering speed.

There's no guarantee we will make it to a rebooted, regenerative model of capitalism, as systemic risk becomes manifest through fires, drought, floods, ecosystem destruction, and deep inequality worldwide. The good news, however, is that a changing global zeitgeist means communities worldwide, from the wealthiest to the most vulnerable, poverty-stricken ones, are 'feeling change and demanding change'. The time for sustainable development is upon us, although the hurdles – political, economic, social, and technical – are formidable against an unforgiving planetary clock.

Nineteen years after it was coined, how did ESG come to sit in a maelstrom of fierce political jousting in the USA, and other countries, as to whether it represented a woke capitalist brake on free markets and business dynamism or legitimate thinking on new risk–reward dynamics underpinning capitalism? This is a complex tale I can only touch upon here.

In an utterly tabloid sense, I believe we are just coming out of the Klondike Gold Rush phase of ESG (2017–23), where the spade sellers, rope brokers, bar owners, brothel owners, and coffin makers were coining money out of the acronym rather than the true sustainability and impact miners themselves – those investors, entrepreneurs, and smart communities delivering value. If the gold rush metaphor holds, my sense is that authenticity and actual ESG delivery will dominate the next decade. From rating agencies, through private equity investors and on to large asset owners, the embedding of ESG thinking into prudential oversight bodies and into both regional and national capital market disciplines will drive authenticity. The acronym may change – this does not really matter – but the risk and rewards of a new political economy in formation will remain.

Daniel Cash's timely book pivots around the importance of signalling theory to the nascent and evolving field of ESG ratings. From the humblest of beginnings, ESG could be framed as a 'hit or miss' signalling theory to the complex global investment chain. In 2004, we had zero idea where ESG would end up, but we were determined to change the investment conversation so that evolving systemic risks – climate, ecosystems destruction, extreme global inequality, social injustice – were seen as material and relevant to fiduciary duty, as well as investment policy and investment decision-making. Nor was ESG just about risk: from the outset our thinking was that if you understand new, evolving, converging risks well, then the investment and business worlds would have a better understanding of the multi-trillion-dollar sustainability markets emerging from clean energy, through regenerative agriculture and on to resilient infrastructure and so much more besides. ESG was and always has been both sides of the risk–reward coin.

The resulting story is worthy of a feature film as a small, forward-looking group of asset managers, supported by an under-resourced team of UN officials, consultants and interns, tipped their cap at global finance and investment and said, 'OK – let's change the conversation.' I believe we succeeded.

From November 2000 on in UNEP FI, the seed of an idea germinated and that stemmed from a belief that no matter how noble and well-intentioned ethical investing, socially responsible investment and corporate social respon-sibility were, they would never mobilise the multi-trillions to materially impact the broad sustainability agenda. This complex agenda, linking devel-opment, economics and environment, emerged after the 1972 UN Stockholm Conference on Human Development and was then formally christened as sus-tainable development by the 1987 UN Brundtland Commission, named after the true force of nature, Gro Harlem Brundtland, a former Norwegian prime minister. Sustainable development remains a fast-evolving agenda, perhaps poorly understood by the broader population, with complex converging sys-temic risks on one side and the prospect of new industries underpinning a shift to regenerative capitalism on the reward side.

To gain traction, the UNEP FI team needed to use the thinking, language, and creativity of mainstream investment and finance to even start the conver-sation with an often impenetrable community. Our fundamental question was, why is responsible investment financially material and aligned with evolving fiduciary duty in a changing, complex world?

As we moved into 2002–03, my UNEP FI core team's thinking – Yuki Yasui, Ken Maguire, Gordon Haggart, James Gifford, Jacob Malthouse, Trevor Bowden, and Philip Walker – settled on the fact that the vision, goals, and objectives of the UN itself were strongly aligned with those of the largest, long-term asset owners, the pension funds, insurance reserves and sovereign funds. In short, those elements at the very heart of the UN mission – secu-rity, development, environment, and humanitarian response – defined what long-term asset owners with a duty to protect, and ideally grow, capital for their beneficiaries needed. If the world is 'going to hell in a hand basket', it's hard for markets to work and for investors to make that mid- to long-term return to protect pools of retirement capital and insurance reserves.

There were three anchoring elements that were needed to allow ESG and then the PRI to take flight in the mid-2000s, and they included:

- In 2002–03, UNEP FI persuaded some of the world's largest asset man-agers to provide free, investment analyst quality research, exploring how occupational health, safety and environment (OHSE) issues affected equity pricing across multiple business and industry sectors. To our surprise, just by asking as the UN, we received at UNEP FI 1,100 pages of research from multiple asset managers. By May 2004, OHSE had morphed into ESG in a development described below.
- In 2004–05, we initiated a discussion with the late and great Professor Paul Q. Watchman and his team at Magic Circle legal firm Freshfields Bruckhaus Deringer, exploring ESG in the context of fiduciary law in the nine major capital markets. By October 2005, this yielded a 150-page legal interpretation, know universally as The Freshfields Report, which became

a critical anchor providing legal legitimacy for the financial materiality and fiduciary relevance of ESG issues in the world's largest capital markets. At the time, Watchman and I postulated that Freshfields was like 'rolling a metaphorical hand grenade' into those who held on to the investment belief and status quo in terms of fiduciary duty being premised purely on profit maximisation. The intense debate continues today. The UK Law Commission validated Watchman's interpretation in 2011.

- Through 2005–06, working with the UN Global Compact, we engaged with UN Secretary General (UNSG) Kofi Annan's team, which resulted in the magisterial diplomat launching the UNPRI as he opened the US capital markets on 27 April 2006, in the iconic Opening Bell Ceremony at the New York Stock Exchange. On that day, 53 institutional investors, representing US$4 trillion in assets, signed the six principles and 39 advocated actions making up the UNPRI. The institutions backing the PRI in 2023 are 100 times that and the assets have multiplied by more than 30 times.

In short, by 2005 we had the investment research, the solid legal basis, and in 2006 we had the glorious theatre of a UNSG opening the US capital markets, to launch a novel collaborative partnership that 17 years on is backed by more than 5,100 institutional investors representing some US$121 trillion in assets. At the simplest level, that US$121 trillion is the signal to the markets that ESG is relevant, material, timely, and a powerful lens with which to view risk and reward in a changing, challenging, complex world.

From all the work towards ESG and the PRI, two footnotes of colour continue to resonate with me from a dynamic period some 20 years ago.

It was May 2004 in my fifth-floor UN office in Environment House, Geneva, and it was decision time. Five of us knocked backwards and forwards whether the 'acronym' should be GES, SGE, GSE, or whatever combination of those three letters which might work. Governance – the G – is obviously key, as a company or investor gets that wrong and the environmental and social elements will never settle effectively in the organisation. The discussion roamed backwards and forwards that day. It was a robust conversation amongst the core team which had relentlessly driven forward for two years, with barely any resources, the project to link materiality, fiduciary duty, and the evolving concept of responsible investment. My instincts as a UK tabloid journalist from the 1980s kicked in: start with governance and you lose people out of the gate, too technocratic, too elitist; environment is sexier, touchable, more directly meaningful for a broader range of people, and some embryonic metrics were already evolving; and social is by far and wide the most difficult for investors and business to deal with. Critically, social – the S – is most likely to be flicked off the end of any acronym by Milton Friedmanesque lobbyists. The S needed ultimate protection.

So, place E up front, weld S in the middle, and the all-important G to anchor and lock everything in. ESG was born. A personal reason, not often voiced but true, nevertheless, is that my two young sons were then at the Geneva English School (GES) where I was on the board, so GES could not be considered no matter how obvious it was. So, there was no science behind the final coining of ESG, but rather journalistic instinct of how important the ordering of words and the sound created are. ESG as easy as 1,2,3 or A,B,C.

Perhaps the most important foundation stone in the evolution of ESG and the UNPRI was set in place on 7 July 2005. Following up on immaculate work by the UNEP FI team, I had flown to London from Geneva on the earliest morning flight to meet for the first time with the late and great Professor Paul Q. Watchman, an academic and corporate lawyer of great vision based on a profound sense of social and environmental justice, joined by London-based team member Trevor Bowden. As we sat, early morning, in Paul's Fleet Street office at law firm Freshfields Bruckhaus Deringer, discussing what would become of his defining legal interpretation of ESG and fiduciary law in the nine major capital markets, unbeknownst to us was that, as we spoke, tragically 56 people were to lose their lives on that day or subsequently as four suicide bombers desecrated the city. This was a day never to be forgotten for all the very worst of reasons. Paul Watchman's lifetime of work will never be forgotten for all the right reasons as we strive to transform 250 years of extractive capitalism into a regenerative model yielding the sustainable world this great man believed in.

So, where does almost 20 years of ESG and 18 for the UNPRI leave us?

I have argued that ESG is at its most effective when deployed by investment institutions, companies, and public agencies, at three levels:

1. systemic (understanding how converging complex systemic risks impact your sector/organisation);
2. strategic (how you compare and position on ESG with peers in your broad sector); and
3. operational (how you assess, prioritise, and enact ESG house cleaning to avoid greenwashing and actually 'walk the talk').

Now, that three-layered approach is not cheap and, yet, the benefits it builds in terms of culture influencing organisational resilience and receptiveness to change and recognising new investment and commercial opportunities in a volatile, changing, uncertain world are, essentially, the purpose of ESG. It's about culture change for organisations based on refreshed, forward-looking governance exploring the future world we are moving into, not the navel-gazing retrospective approach examining the risk datasets that defined the 20th century.

So, let's have a look at some of the systemic challenges such a deep ESG assessment would reveal for investors, companies, and public agencies serious about sustainability impact to reduce risk while delivering positive impact coupled with return on critical global goals.

Significant changes are needed for the delivery of a fair and affordable transition to sustainability in the 21st century. At current rates, the UN's 17 Sustainable Development Goals (SDGs) – scheduled as a serious framework for delivery between 2016 and 2030 – will not be delivered until 2082.[1] Post-Covid-19, some predict SDG delivery will shift to the early 2090s, perhaps 2100. The annual gap for financing required to deliver the goals has jumped from US$2.5 trillion (pre-Covid-19) to US$3.7 trillion.[2] The risk of not addressing sustainable development issues is an enormous constraint on economic development, which could threaten system stability, and have profoundly negative consequences for governments, communities, businesses, and investors.

The sustainability financing challenge accelerated after the global Covid-19 pandemic exposed the depth of inequality with socioeconomic dislocation for the most vulnerable communities. The links between key drivers of social deprivation with those of environmental destruction[3] have been further highlighted, notably in the 46 least developed countries (LDCs) as well as within deep pockets of poverty, which are often located in communities dependent on agricultural value chains. The Financing for Development Initiative (FfDI) is an important multilateral policy response which recognises that the pandemic exacerbated challenges, and advocates for early action to safeguard against the most extreme impacts on those left furthest behind.

Concerns about climate change and how these manifest challenges may translate in policy terms to environmental restrictions to trade – unduly impacting the most vulnerable communities in the LDCs and middle-income economies – are growing. In this regard, there is growing attention on how countries, notably LDCs, can protect the inherent, financial, and nutritional value embedded in their territorial supply chains for the benefit of vulnerable communities.[4]

Efforts to align investments with climate goals and social good have been building for a decade but have taken off in the past few years. According to data from Morningstar, assets in sustainable funds grew 53% year-on-year to US$2.74 trillion in 2021.[5] ESG-linked debt issuance more than tripled in 2021 to US$190 billion. Sustainability-related equity fund flows also rose to US$25 billion, bringing total assets under management to nearly US$150 billion. ESG investments now make up almost 18% of foreign financing for emerging markets excluding China, quadruple the average for recent years.[6] The period of deep ESG 'political contention' (2022–23) has seen the speed and growth of ESG uptake by the investment community drop off while it remains a critical nascent block of deepening capital.

However, there is great disparity across our global capital markets in terms of their depth, liquidity, and the flow of investment into those markets outside a very concentrated set of OECD countries – principally, those with just 10% of the total number of exchanges control 80% of assets in exchanges. Unpeeling the statistics further reveals both the opportunities and challenges for effective flows of finance to deliver the SDGs to countries outside of the developed economies of the G7/G20. Before the Covid-19 pandemic, the annual SDG finance gap reached US$2.5 trillion. The pandemic widened the gap to between US$3.7 trillion and US$4.2 trillion annually, as estimates show that developing countries witnessed a US$700 billion drop in external private finance along with a gap of US$1 trillion in public spending on Covid-19 recovery measures compared with advanced economies. The pandemic exposed the fragility of our global system to profound shocks, with the severest impacts falling on the most vulnerable communities. With world gross product falling by 4.3% in 2020, it was estimated that upward of 120 million people fell into extreme poverty, with an additional 270 million people facing acute food shortages by the year's end.[7] These developments saw significant backsliding in SDG1 (no poverty) and SDG2 (zero hunger).

While the dual climate–biodiversity crisis has captured global policy attention, the renewed focus on social challenges catalysed by the FfDI in the era of Covid-19 and beyond has captured the severity of financial impacts on communities worldwide and the urgent need for debt relief triggered by the pandemic. It also started to reframe our understanding of converging systemic risks with clear strengthening of links between climate, ecosystems stress, and both social and economic dislocation.

In today's financialised global economy, markets are the principal means through which financial systems allocate capital. The building blocks of our current global market system, which have spurred rapid development for some while leaving many communities behind, need re-engineering to deliver positive impact on a global scale, contribute to the foundations for a regenerative political economy, and reflect rapidly changing contexts. The change can be captured in some overarching trends, such as the demographics megatrend where global population is set to reach 10.9 billion by 2100 while the demographics are shifting towards ageing.[8] In addition to demographic trends, the labour market is also seeing rising levels of automation, which could be directed to have net positive impact. The climate crisis will also have economic and social impacts on forced migration and strains on food global value chains. Another trend is the increasing poverty and income inequality within and between countries, which was exacerbated by the pandemic.

As our goals and the challenges facing the global community are interconnected, the time has come to fully integrate the SDGs into the global financial
system to effectively deliver country-level sustainability benefits. The SDGs
offer a holistic approach to development that considers the interdependence of
human and natural systems. The integrated development system established by
the UN SDGs would require adjusting incentives and penalties for the markets,
and ensure adequate supervision and compliance are essential to fully integrate
the SDGs.

To open a flow of finance for sustainable development, the world needs
supportive investment platforms based on the financial systemisation of the
SDG framework, speeding optimised allocation of capital to sustainability,
thereby maximising the delivery of the goals and rewarding key stakeholders.
Equally, the need at country level to enhance capacity and expertise, as well
as supportive policy environments, to create investable ecosystems yielding
bankable sustainable investment projects is fundamental.

The diverse global business community, and the supply and value chains
which interconnect the largest firms with the smallest, need access to a stand-
ardised and systemised sustainable financial system anchored by the SDGs.
Incompleteness and inconsistency in sustainability-related disclosures pose
a major challenge to market fairness, efficiency, transparency, and integrity.
Without the requisite information, firms may be unable to verify that they are
pursuing genuinely sustainable investment strategies. They may also be unable
to demonstrate to consumers the sustainability-related characteristics of their
products and performance against their stated objectives. Securities regulators
and capital market authorities' objectives include protecting investors, maintaining fair, efficient, and transparent markets, and seeking to address systemic
risks, as well as supporting market integrity by requiring transparency and
disclosure of information that is material to investment decisions. However,
frequently, sustainability reporting is not integrated into issuers' periodic
reporting structure but is instead treated as a separate and often siloed reporting
activity within companies.

A United Nations report[9] from 2011 noted:

> fundamental aspects of international accounting systems and capital market dis-
> ciplines, as well as our understanding of fiduciary responsibility in investment
> policymaking and investment decision-making, will need to evolve to fully integrate
> a broader range of environmental, social and governance (ESG) factors than takes
> place at present. Without these changes, the pricing signals and incentives that
> would support the transition to a green economy will remain weak.

Increasingly, global investors,[10] including the largest asset owners which
are considered as universal investors,[11] are aligning with the sentiments in
the decade-old UN paper. Evolving standards and regulatory changes under

way at global, regional, and national levels mean investors are obligated to understand, report on, and disclose better the impacts and consequences of their allocations to the real economy, as well as the societal and environmental context which supports these allocations.

Decades of research demonstrate that sustainability thinking at all levels of governance can catalyse the flow of finance at scale while helping to manage and mitigate negative policy trade-offs across the developmental, economic, and environmental aspects of our evolving political economies. The July 2015 Addis Ababa Action Agenda created 'a strong foundation to support the implementation of the UN's 2030 Agenda for Sustainable Development'[12] by aligning financing flows and policies with economic, social, and environmental priorities. Research in 2021 highlighted that 'environment-human linkages affect the outcome of the vast majority of SDGs'.[13]

Accelerating the alignment of investment and management decision-making across the policymaking, capital markets, and business worlds with deep sustainability thinking focused on positive global impact will be transformational. The ability to catalyse clean global financial flows, while de-risking and freeing pools of domestic capital in the developing and least developed economies, will empower the implementation of the SDGs.[14] Well-resourced and targeted sustainability action will translate into localisation and delivery of the SDGs for each country worldwide in a manner that will define the success of the 2030 Agenda.[15] The world's largest multinational corporations are often the subject of intense focus with respect to sustainability and impact. However, the critical sustainability role of micro, small and medium-sized enterprises (MSMEs), making up 90% of all firms and accounting, on average, for 70% of total employment and 50% of gross domestic product (GDP),[16] cannot be overestimated.

The SDGs provide a blueprint to understand the opportunities associated with the emergence of new industries, businesses, and new methods of financing a sustainable economy. The SDGs create a pathway for a new sustainability supporting approaches to government and broader public sector procurement practices, as well as targeted policy interventions to incentivise and accelerate the uptake of sustainable finance and responsible investment approaches by mainstream investment and business. As the Business Commission on Sustainable Development argues, 'Contributing to and achieving the SDGs offer a compelling growth strategy for businesses and the world economy as a whole.'[17] If the SDGs were pursued in 'food and agriculture, cities, energy and materials, and health and well-being'[18] alone it could increase the global economy by 26%,[19] unlocking a US$12 trillion annual business opportunity. The potential and scaling of sustainability-aligned fixed-income products, at the sovereign, municipal, and corporate levels, will play an increasingly important role in financing a just transition, as illustrated by the exponential growth of the global climate bond markets[20] in recent years.

The challenges to ensure flows of clean capital at scale and a rapid transformation in the market and corporate decision-making are manifold. These challenges, in part, stem from a global financial system which is clearly suboptimal for true sustainability and undermines the evidence-based scientific boundaries for planetary and societal health, which are increasingly coming into a sharper focus. We know that increased capital or finance alone will not automatically yield a positive global impact, nor address the consequences of unfettered development through growth at any cost. There remains a wide gap between the current system's focus on financial materiality and the true needs of sustainability, where public interest materiality would benefit from an equal footing. There needs to be a much clearer and more readily understood common global narrative for the concept of double materiality.[21]

It is crucial for the global financial system to address a cascading torrent of converging systemic risks, covering manmade and natural systems, while also 'achieving sustainable growth, environmental protection and poverty reduction'.[22] The UN SDGs help us understand the complex, interconnected, and accelerating nature of converging global systemic risks, including but not limited to climate volatility, ecosystems destruction, social dislocation, food insecurity, conflict, and inequality, which deepens environmental and societal fragility. Consequences are always felt most directly at the local level in an already unfolding disturbing dystopian tapestry impacting the marginalised and those left furthest behind. Critical sustainability questions, in part answered by the G20 Sustainable Finance Roadmap (SFR), should continue to be addressed with coordinated responses by international organisations working with national agencies on a prioritised basis.

Strong indicators across governments, markets, industrial and business sectors, as well as within the investment and financial communities, suggest positive sustainability change has never been more conceivable. There is a need to see a refinement of accounting, reporting, and disclosure mechanisms to adjust incentives to more directly align with sustainability to drive change in financing, investment, businesses, and capital markets, as well as better re-engineering of other public and private practices to embed regenerative characteristics. The utilisation of decision-relevant information and the data governance architecture facilitating effective use will be important in this transition. Therefore, to deliver the SDGs, it is critical to connect data sources across the system (including administrative data) and at different levels of the international system. Aggregation of data to understand system-wide effects, with governments being able to include private sector contributions, will enhance understanding and decision-making. At the same time, the challenges around effective disaggregation of data to ensure an adequate focus on the last mile and the needs of the most vulnerable communities is required to identify gaps in SDG delivery.

There is a need for a balance between a systemic shift through cohesive global action while accelerating national adoption to ensure that the financial system, in the mid to long term, can support a form of sustainable growth which respects environmental and societal boundaries. For greater sustainability-aligned public accountability, policymakers, regulators, and standard-setters need to weave a robust, while transparent, thread between both public and private internal management accounting and decision-making strategies with external reporting and disclosure. These three important disciplines of market and public interest, refocused and well calibrated for positive impact, will help achieve sustainable growth through improved/innovative collaboration, while creating a path to decision-making aligned with sustainability as a norm in business and investment. It will also create a culture and marketplace where reporting and disclosure is normalised across countries.

Paul Clements-Hunt
Founder, The Blended Capital Group
Director, Mishcon Purpose, Mishcon de Reya LLP

NOTES

1. Social Progress Imperative, '2020 Social Progress Index,' Social Progress Imperative, Washington DC.
2. OECD (2020), Global Outlook on Financing for Sustainable Development 2021: A New Way to Invest for People and Planet, OECD Publishing, Paris, https://dx .doi. org/10.1787/e3c30a9aen
3. *See* https:// www .un .org/ sus tainablede velopment/ blog/ 2016/ 05/ rate -of -environmental-damage-increasing-across-planet-but-still-time-to-reverse-worst -impacts/
4. *See* https:// www .nepad .org/ event/ un -food -systems -summit -territorial -governance-sustainable-food-systems
5. *See* https://on.ft.com/3Jv24KT
6. *See* https://blogs.imf.org/2022/03/01/sustainable-finance-in-emerging-markets -is-enjoying-rapid-growth-but-may-bring-risks/
7. *See* https://www.un.org/zh/node/81536
8. *See* https:// www .un .org/ development/ desa/ en/ news/ population/ world -population-prospects-2019.html
9. United Nations Environment Program, Towards a Green Economy, UNEP 2011, https:// su stainabledevelopment .un .org/ content/ documents/ 126GER_synthesis _en.pdf
10. See United Nations supported Principles for Responsible Investment, www.unpri .org
11. United Nations supported Principles for Responsible Investment, Macro risks: Universal ownership, 13 October 2017, https:// www .unpri .org/ sustainable

-development -goals/ the -sdgs -are -an -unavoidable -consideration -for -universal -owners/306.article

12. Ibid.
13. 'Towards understanding interactions between sustainable development goals: the role of environment-human linkages,' 1 April 2020, https:// link .springer .com/article/10.1007/s11625-020-00799-6
14. *See* United Nations Development Programme, SDGs in Action, https:// www .undp.org/sustainable-development-goals
15. *See* United Nations, Department of Economic and Social Affairs, Sustainable Development, Transforming our World: the 2030 Agenda for Sustainable Development, https://sdgs.un.org/2030agenda
16. *See* https://www.un.org/en/observances/micro-small-medium-businesses-day
17. 'Better Business Better World' report by the Business Commission on Sustainable Development's (BCSD).
18. Business and Sustainable Development Commission, http://businesscommission .org/
19. Council on Financial Relations, https:// www .cfr .org/ womens -participation -in -global-economy/
20. *See* https://www.climatebonds.net/2021/08/climate-bonds-updates-2021-green -forecast-half-trillion-latest-h1-figures-signal-new-surge
21. *See* https://www.lse.ac.uk/granthaminstitute/news/double-materiality-what-is-it -and-why-does-it-matter/
22. Achieving Sustainable Growth, Wealth Creation and Poverty Reduction, presentation to the UN Secretary General's High Level Panel on Sustainability by Rt Hon Gordon Brown MP, Sunday 18 September 2011.

1. Introduction to *ESG Rating Agencies and Financial Regulation*

How do we balance trust with responsibility? Trust, conceptually, is something which we can all relate to and is foundational, or even fundamental, to human existence. How do you trust somebody that you do not know? It is perhaps impossible to fully answer that question, or fully trust somebody or something else, but, if one wants to invest resources, then an element of trust is fundamentally required. Yet, many relationships in the modern world bring with them a level of responsibility that then intrinsically affects the dynamic of apportioning trust. This book is based on these inherent human questions.

Many seemingly complex interactions in the modern financial space can be boiled down to very simplistic concepts like those above. For example, investment in the millions and billions of dollars, pounds, euro, yen, or renminbi is dependent upon an investor trusting that they will likely receive their investment back. However, the world has changed in recent generations in that, whereas once you or I may have invested personally, quite often now we would do so through an intermediary – an institutional investor. Such investors now span entire economies, managing more assets than many countries. However, at its core, the institutional investor is bound by a simple relationship – that between the principal (you or I) and the agent (the investment management team). That principal–agent dynamic affects everything around it and is the reason that the modern financial marketplace has evolved in the way that it has.

For example, Chapter 2 focuses on the credit rating sector, and that sector is a great place to start asking serious and often uncomfortable questions. We will be introduced to the sector in great detail in Chapter 2, but a common question asked of the industry is just how the agencies (a) managed to perform in the transgressive manner that they did in the lead-up to the Global Financial Crisis of 2007/08, but then (b) how they have managed to thrive since, rather than capitulate under pressure the sector had never experienced before. The chapter and the book will describe how, and position the credit rating sector in a technical assessment first, and then a more existential one throughout. The concept of private business is an underlying theme that dominates the book's understanding as the inter-relationships between all those parties invested in the demand for and supply on investment capital. The credit rating agencies' critical position between all of those in this network is revealed and provided as an exemplar for understanding better the nascent ESG rating sector.

To understand better the environment that the ESG rating agencies are currently operating within, the book makes a diversion and focuses on the interconnection between the concept of ESG and the law in Chapter 3. It does this in order to understand the complexities of the movement of ESG and its position in relation to modern business practices. Ultimately, even though it is certainly debatable, ESG as a movement is concerned with making business act in a different, more progressive manner, and that attempt to evolve the culture of business is bringing the concept in direct conflict with many of the laws that have already been established to control and guide the culture of business. To that end, the chapter works through two of the key legal considerations where the concept of ESG is having the most impact: disclosure and duty. By reviewing leading developments in these two fields, the chapter is able to understand the varying intricate positions that the ESG rating agencies can take with regards to aiding and assisting with key business processes like that witnessed within the agent–principal relationship that governs so much of the modern business environment.

On that basis the book moves into Chapter 4, which is where we get introduced to the ESG rating agencies in all their glory. The growth of the sector is detailed alongside the developing dynamics that are associated with that growth. Those developing dynamics are covered in reviewing and critiquing the range of issues that have been identified in the literature, amongst trade bodies and by regulators and legislators. With an array of issues being identified, the outlook for the ESG rating agencies looks negative, but the chapter then breaks down each of the major regulatory and legislative endeavours that have sprung up to resolve the issues and make the sector more useful to its many stakeholders. Detailed breakdowns of the IOSCO call for action, European regulation that has been proposed, Indian regulation that has been enacted, and developments from Japan, the United Kingdom, and the United States are all provided. This allows the book to provide an up-to-the-minute critique of developments in the sector and provide a launchpad off of which the last substantive chapter can ask significant questions.

Chapter 5 injects the theoretical lens that is required in order to answer the prevailing questions the book has put forward. Understanding the applicability of signalling theory and the concept of a natural oligopoly provides the book with everything it needs to understand the peculiarities within the credit rating sector and the reasoning for the astounding level of criticism being directed towards the ESG rating sector. The chapter manages to frame the issues within one key understanding, which is directly related to the *role* that a rater plays within a given system. Key foundational concepts are dissected, like informational asymmetry, to better understand the centralised and critical role that a rater plays.

Ultimately, the book seeks to answer questions which are related to things that often go unsaid. In the financial sense, words like oligopoly carry a negative connotation that a lot of stakeholders cannot ever mention, like the state. But, when analysed properly, a system of delivering critical services to the financial system moreover needs to be understood properly and, sometimes, difficult or uncomfortable concepts need to be openly discussed. This is what this book does. It provides you, the reader, with the reasoning as to why the rater prevails irrespective of their conduct. It provides an answer as to why the entire marketplace seems desperate and determined to have ESG rating agencies become better, despite there being no evidence of their ability to rise to the challenge. It gives you questions, and then answers to fundamental components within the financial system. As the movement of ESG grows ever larger, those answers are needed.

2.   Liability in the credit rating space

1.   INTRODUCTION

Every corporate entity will be concerned with the concept of liability. There are libraries of books on the liability of almost every sector imaginable, but what is often overlooked is the concept of 'liability' in particular. There have been a handful of key treatises, like White's 1985 book *Grounds of Liability*,[1] but intertwined within the concept of liability are humanistic and also philosophical concepts like fear, anticipation, anxiety, strategy, and a host of other almost carnal issues. In the field of *ratings*, almost irrespective of the actual form that takes, these core aspects listed above are all present and influence the thinking of those tasked with guiding the institutions that produce *ratings*. In this chapter, those fundamental influences will all be revealed as we seek to understand better the inherent relationship between the concept of rating, and the concept of liability.

Why it is important to understand the relationship between those two concepts may be immediately clear to some, but not to others. It is hardly controversial to suggest that a private company is concerned with its liability. However, how that concern manifests itself and the impact it has on the operations of the private entity is a critical consideration. Also, whether that 'fear' is witnessed in all elements of how a business operates is important to understand. As we shall see in this chapter, the credit rating agencies have an almost cultural aversion to liability, yet partake in activities which propel them directly into the crosshairs of parties that only have litigation as a way of remedying the harms caused by those activities. Arguably, it is perhaps this laser focus on one's exposure to liability which allows one to partake in such potentially harmful practices; this very sentiment lies underneath this chapter and, in truth, the whole book.

Yet, it is not merely the case that credit rating agencies are adept at protecting themselves from liability and that this is the only lesson to learn. The wider reality is much more important and is systemic in nature. We shall see in this chapter, and throughout the book, that there are power dynamics at play which determine what can and cannot be done from a regulatory/legislative standpoint. Later in the chapter we will be introduced to the concept of the *natural oligopoly*, which is so critical in our understanding. This is because, whilst understanding the concept of an oligopoly reveals a large number of truths, the concept of a *natural* oligopoly expands that understanding further still. When we pair that with the analysis in the last chapter, which looks at the application of signalling theory to the concept of ratings generally, the power game is revealed in full. It is argued in this book that it is only from within those parameters that the fields of credit and ESG ratings can be truly understood.

One of the main reasons for this book's development is to take advantage of a moment in time. The ESG rating space is in its infancy, and the regulation/ control of the space is even younger still and being actively developed at the time of writing. This is very unique. In the credit rating space, the reality was much different. The act of producing ratings, in a broad sense, first belonged to the trade communities in industrial Britain, and the concept was then adapted by the large British financing houses seeking to take advantage of the expansion in the antebellum United States. Whilst the trade societies needed to protect against fraud, the large financing houses needed to improve the probability of credit being repaid in a land where they were not present, so they utilised the knowledge of local business leaders and developed relatively complex networks of 'reporters' who opined on the standing of businesspeople in different regions. As the United States grew and business grew across the burgeoning country, the need for a market solution to the market-based problem of informational asymmetry in relation to trading resulted in the first commercialised agency in 1835. Whilst that first agency did not survive, it was picked up by another entity just six years later and that agency thrived (for several reasons, which we will unpick shortly) and became what is today Dun & Bradstreet. Based upon those successes, notable figures like John Moody and Henry Varnum Poor developed evolved offerings that married the concept to a simplistic signalling method which became central to the ever-expanding commercial marketplace that dominated their world, and continues to dominate our world today. The reason for providing you with this whistle-stop tour of the genealogy of 'ratings' in the modern era is to show the difference with what is happening in the ESG rating space. The credit rating model spans back hundreds of years in reality, so any control of it would naturally come afterwards, not before. The courts reactively considered the concept of libel and its application to what the early agencies were doing, and the early securities regulators of the 1930s in the US considered, loosely, the purpose and role of the early credit rating agencies. It would not be until 2005/06 that the first formal legislation would be enacted with the credit rating agencies in mind, some 30 years after the Securities and Exchange Commission (SEC) had sought to insert itself somewhat into the field by forming the 'Nationally Recognised Statistical Rating Organisation' (NRSRO) moniker so as to develop a registration system for those that already existed. The 2005/06 laws failed because the horse had already bolted from the stable in relation to the Global Financial

Crisis (GFC), but the Dodd-Frank Act of 2010, itself reacting to the GFC, was the US's first full-scale attempt at controlling the credit rating agencies. In the EU, three major regulations starting in 2009 (and then 2011 and 2013) were the first-ever European attempts to control the rating agencies – that is, even in relation to the formal birth of the credit rating agencies with John Moody's first company, full regulation 110 years later. In relation to the wider geneal-ogy of commercialised ratings, it is 169 years.

Today, in the ESG rating space, the opportunity is very different. There both exists the opportunity to start from the ground up and institute meaningful standards, and also the opportunity to implement the learning from the failures of regulating an industry that is almost exactly the same. This rarely happens regulatorily speaking, and it presents legislators and regulators with great opportunity, but serious problems. This is because, upon reflection, a lot of the Dodd-Frank Act and European regulations' aims have not been met, at all. In fact, it is not a stretch to say that large parts of those initiatives have failed. If that is the case, then trusting the transition to ESG regulating to be a smooth affair is difficult. In order to make that transition as sustainable as possible, this book suggests that only by engaging with the *reality* of the situation can the ESG regulators around the world achieve success that is scalable and sus-tainable. Short-term regulatory 'wins' and attacking the lowest hanging fruit, regulatorily speaking, is short-sighted but attractive to regulators. Instead, there is a need to focus on the underlying issues, articulate what is possible and what is not, and then develop strategies to truly achieve the objectives that the regulators ought to be pursuing. In this chapter we will learn about these underlying facets in relation to the credit rating industry so that the challenge facing the ESG rating regulators becomes clearer.

2.   A HISTORY OF LIABILITY AWARENESS IN THE CREDIT RATING INDUSTRY

I, as an author, have endeavoured throughout my career to fundamentally attach the trajectories of the credit reference and credit rating agencies, as a handful of other scholars have done also. I have shown in other works that there are clear connections between the two industries, so much so that we can see it as one larger direction of travel.[2] The shared learnings and cultures between the two industries, in addition to the familial connections between leaders of both industries, displays, to me at least, the shared lineage. In this section, we will delve into this shared lineage to understand whether the liability-related questions being posed today have answers rooted in the past. What will be revealed is that the issue of liability, and then synergistically how the agencies have dealt with that exposure to liability, has always been at the forefront of the industries' concerns. Given the clear connection between the credit rating industry and the new ESG rating industry, which I have also portrayed in a recent work,[3] the same can be said for the ESG rating industry too. All of this has direct implications for those tasked with controlling the new industry.

As briefly hinted at in the introduction to this chapter, the trajectory of the concept of what we may call today *rating* is formed out of the core need to address a distinctly human problem: how can you trust somebody you do not know? This is an oversimplification of the concept of informational asymmetry, which describes the process whereby one entity knows more about something than the other, and potentially can exploit that knowledge gap. The history of trying to resolve this problem, at least commercially, is essentially the story of 'ratings'. Yet, we need to consistently remember these core issues when we analyse and assess the concept of rating because, forgetting to do so, even for a moment, can lead to significant misunderstandings.

The early credit rating agencies took inspiration from the groundwork developed by the credit reporting agencies, like the Mercantile Agency and the Bradstreet Company. Those credit reporting agencies themselves took inspiration from a range of sources. One source of inspiration was the trade-protection societies that were developed in the UK to guard against the abusers of the credit system across the UK. However, there are reasons why the trade-protection society model was not simply just transplanted to the American frontier, as explained by Olegario:

> Trade protection societies based on the British model also did not become the norm in the United States, even in places such as New York City, where one might have expected to find them. A few attempts to establish such groups were made, but the arrangements did not last. The less established nature of trade in the United States, the high mobility of its population within a vast geographic territory, the high churn among businesses, and competition among sellers militated against the formation of stable networks.[4]

With the trade-protection version of resolving commercial informational asymmetry not being suited to the American experience, there was another option. The large financing house of the Baring Brothers had sought to resolve their own asymmetrical problem by employing special agents to act on their behalf and review the businesspeople in the United States who could be trusted to extend credit to from afar. Hidy describes how:

> during the years after the Napoleonic Wars London merchant bankers, including Baring Brothers and Company, faced new complexities in the management of their business. Among the new problems was to find a satisfactory means of selected trustworthy correspondents... in the final analysis, the success of these great lenders and brokers of credit depended in large measure upon the safety and reliability of their clients in America.

To decrease the risk that the banking houses faced, they developed close relationships with leading businesspeople who were able to utilise their experience and deep networks to build extensive compendiums on the reliability of businesspeople across mostly Eastern seaboard-based businesses and businesspeople. As Hidy continues:

> As the Barings understood the term, a correspondent to be reliable must be an accurate judge of the currents of business, must be intensely interested in and devoted to his business operations, must have a capital adequate to his transactions, must be prudent, and above all must be thoroughly honest. Accordingly, in October, 1829, during an extended journey of survey of American business firms and operations, Thomas Baring signed a contract with Thomas Wren Ward, a retired, well-to-do merchant from Boston and personal friend of Bates, to the effect that the latter should act as special resident agent of Baring Brothers and Company in North America... From 1829 to 1853 he rated several thousand American business men of all ranks and types, whether or not they asked for credit from his London principals.[5]

However, this second option was also not appropriate for scaling in the early United States. Olegario explains why this was when she says that:

> None of these alternative models, however, presented a viable solution within the American context. Hiring special agents as Barings did was too expensive for nearly all American firms. Banks were of limited use because banking in the United States was highly fragmented during the nineteenth century (and for most of the twentieth). Branch banking was largely prohibited, which limited their potential for transmitting information across large distances. Conflicts of interest, such as the need to preserve client confidentiality, further diminished the willingness of banks to function as credit-reporting institutions.[6]

The uniqueness of America in the early 19th century meant that a bespoke method of resolving the growing problem of informational asymmetry was required. In 1835, the first attempt at commercialising what Ward was doing with the Baring Brothers was attempted, by a New York City-based law firm called Griffen, Cleaveland, and Campbell.[7] The firm used its lawyers and contracted agents around the city to report on the reliability of businesses and businesspeople, just like Ward had done. Yet, the economic unpredictability of the time wiped out the law firm, and with it the first shot at scaling the process of reporting on businesses. Two years later, the collapse of a large New York-based mercantile firm led by Arthur Tappan helped spark the Panic of 1837 and, in response, Congress sought to quell the financial crisis by enacting the National Bankruptcy Act of 1841, 'which, amongst its many facets, appeared to favour the idea of debtors being able to be pardoned for their debts'. At the same time, Arthur Tappan's younger brother Lewis Tappan had purchased the remains of Griffen, Cleaveland, and Campbell's system of reporting on business reliability and when, in the aftermath of launching the

Bankruptcy Act, the business community reacted in horror to what was seen as a 'jubilee' of debts, he launched the Mercantile Agency that offered exactly the same service as the defunct law firm. It mattered little that Congress would repeal the Act just months later; Tappan was now in business and the second attempt at commercialising Ward's system was flourishing in an era dominated by mistrust.[8]

Tappan's Mercantile Agency quickly became central to the growing credit markets in antebellum America. Tappan quickly established branch offices throughout the country and would even manage to operate in the south of the country, which was remarkable given his anti-slavery celebrity (in reality, Tappan outsourced the expansion of the firm to another man – Edward E. Dunbar – and essentially developed a 'Trojan horse' strategy to enable expansion into the south).[9] However, whilst the Mercantile Agency became the dominant force in the reporting industry, almost becoming synonymous with providing the service, its broad usage did not reflect how it was regarded. The reality is much different, and, through the lens of liability, we see the continuation of the first stage of the relationship between ratings and liability that this book will illustrate.

The first instance of resolving informational asymmetry and liability becoming conjoined concepts occurred in the United Kingdom, with the trade-protection societies we discussed earlier. Olegario notes that in 1826, so pre-dating the Mercantile Agency by 17 years, the British case of *Goldstein v. Foss, et al* (1826) was concerned with the legal concept of *privileged communication*. The case centred on the claim by Mr Goldstein that the inclusion of his name within a trade-protection society's circulars labelling him as a person that has engaged in fraudulent activity constituted libel. The court was faced with the question of whether the trade-protection society's circular was protected under the guise of privileged communication, and it subsequently decided that it was not. However, in other cases like *Fleming v. Newton* (1848), the courts found that the circulars could contain anything that was in the public record.[10]

Privileged communication is a legal concept that is applied to a range of different disciplines, with the more obvious being the field of psychiatry, for example. However, in relation to the relationship we are focusing on, a judge in the late 1880s in the United States defined privileged communication by saying that 'a communication is privileged when made in good faith in answer to one having an interest in the information sought'.[11] Perhaps a more useful understanding of the application of this doctrine to the field we are concerned with comes from Flandreau and Mesevage:

American common law—it is argued—gave US judges the flexibility to depart from the legal standard set by Britain, which was adverse to the public circulation of commercial information. US judges saw the necessity of the mercantile agencies' system and ruled so as to allow the agencies' continued existence. This occurred through a generous interpretation of what constituted 'privileged communications' (communications that were protected from liability) using a loophole in libel law known as 'Qualified Privilege.' A 'Qualified Privilege' defense argued that the agencies were 'duty-bound' to issue credit reports: if they were duty-bound, then errors were admissible and it would fall upon the accuser to demonstrate that a factual error had been maliciously made.[12]

So, in moving away from the British approach of guarding against the public circulation of sensitive information, the US courts reveal the early necessity of the services being offered by the credit reporting agencies and provided the necessary legal protection for them to continue offering those services. This is a critical understanding. It allows us to witness the different, sometimes even existential, factors at play when considering the relationship between 'ratings' and 'liability', and it is instructive for us as we seek to understand how the relationship will develop within the ESG era. However, as is usually the case with the world of 'ratings', things are not so simple.

Flandreau and a variety of his colleagues over a number of works have sought to dig into the reality of the facts and figures, and their findings are revealing. It is the common understanding that the US courts sought to extend the protection afforded by the concept of 'qualified privilege' – the sentiment being, as discussed above, that the systemic importance of the agencies trumped any privacy concerns that emanated from their services. Flandreau and his colleagues, however, found that the reality was that the extension of qualified privilege was limited at best, and that the agencies' lawyers knew this. Flandreau and Mesevage go further by stating that 'in fact, the *Macintosh* brief showed that in many cases and for many of the products the agencies distributed, US Judges had not deemed rating an activity protected by Qualified Privilege'.[13] The implications of this are broad. It pours cold water on the linkages that some have put between the legal protections offered by securities regulators in the 1930s, which many have suggested was in continuation of the legal protections offered by the courts to rating and reporting agencies before then. It also raises the question of how the agencies managed to guard against being exposed to a fatal amount of liability, if their products were not legally protected against that liability? Well, as Flandreau and Mesevage say in the early stages of their excellent article:

> In the story we tell, nothing is left of the insistence in the prevailing view on the greater wisdom of US judges who helped the business of transparency to come out on top. Our narrative portrays the conspicuous efforts, by the mercantile agencies, to settle claims, corrupt opponents and lawyers, and thwart individual libel cases, while at the same time using a number of media and paid supporters to organize the narrative that we find in conventional accounts. On the basis of our archival evi-

dence, we thus undertake to revisit the triumph of rating in late-nineteenth-century America. We show that mercantile rating expanded despite judicial opinion, and beyond the boundaries of nineteenth-century tort. We find that resistance to rating was much more deeply entrenched than conventionally admitted, as reflected in the fact that many courts viewed the business model of mercantile rating with skepticism.[14]

This resistance is important, because it sets the scene for the opening monologue in the relationship between commercialised ratings and liability as a concept. In illustrating the sentiment being shown towards the nascent industry, Madison notes how in 1854 the reporting (ratings) business was described as 'an organised system of espionage which, centred in New York, extends its ramifications to every city, village, and school district in the Union'.[15] A judge wrote of the Mercantile Agency that 'its operations are secret, everything is sent out under the garb of confidence, and thus the poisoned arrows which are launched in darkness, may strike down the purest and most solvent in the land; no business man is safe...'.[16]

This attention through the courts and the press led to legislative attempts to curtail the spread of the agencies. In 1873 and 1874, four states in particular introduced bills 'to make the agencies responsible for losses suffered by businessmen as a result of inaccurate credit reports'. Whilst the bills in Missouri, Illinois, and New York died at an early stage of ascension, the bill in Pennsylvania did not. It was entitled 'An Act to Punish Commercial Agents for False Representations of the Business Condition of Certain Persons' with a fine of $1,000 for a representative of an agency 'who shall knowingly, heedlessly, or wilfully exaggerate or misrepresent... the credit, financial responsibility or business condition of any... persons engaged in any commercial business'. The Act even incentivised businesspeople to come forward by stating that half of the fine would be paid to the businessperson in question. However, in demonstrating how the agencies dealt with liability exposure in their early iterations, the actions of one of the senior managers in what was then R.G. Dun & Company – Robert Dun had purchased the Mercantile Agency from the retired Tappan at this point – is illustrative:

> Erastus Wiman, who began his career as a clerk in a branch office, was responsible for the day-to-day operation of R.G. Dun & Company in 1874. To defeat the Pennsylvania attempt at regulation, Wiman directed the preparation of fifty telegrams stating opposition to the bill. He mailed the telegrams to Agency offices in Philadelphia, Pittsburgh, Reading, Allentown, Williamsport, and Erie, where employees gathered signatures from leading businessmen in the area. The Agency also sent form letters to prominent Pennsylvania businessmen, requesting that they write to their legislators opposing the bill. As a result, Wiman later wrote, 'the Senators were fairly overwhelmed with protests against the measure from the biggest men among their constituents in all parts of the State... Never before had

they received so many dispatches, on one subject, from quarters so influential in so short a time.' And, Wiman added, 'This circumstance simply shows what can be done by a little forethought, manipulation, and management in the shape of working-up sentiment in the interest of fair play.'[17]

The reality then is a difficult one to nail down. It is true in one sense that the legal framework designed to protect consumers and citizens failed to adequately constrain the reach and operations of the early reporting agencies. However, it is also true that there are limits to what that legal framework can achieve when the subject is actively strategising to avoid being held account-able. It is somewhat natural to expect this, but it is clear from the examples above (and many more in the literature) that the early reporting agencies were fully focused on doing what was necessary to survive, irrespective of the damage it caused. Yet, putting any sort of moralistic discussion aside, the reality is that the leading agency, and others close to it, avoided debilitating exposure to liability in its formative stages and this allowed the concept of what they were offering to the marketplace to evolve into something almost separate from its host. The more complex business became as the early United States continued to expand, the more important resolving informational asym-metry became, and despite its absolute assault on key values like privacy, the service being offered by the agencies was quickly becoming indispensable. It is on that foundation that the actions of regulators some years later – once the credit rating agencies that would turn into Moody's, S&P, and Fitch start trading and evolving the concept of reporting and rating into one cohesive unit – become pertinent and set the scene for the epitome of the relationship between the concepts of rating and liability in the GFC.

3.   INDUCING RELIANCE OR REACTIONARY REGULATION?

The credit rating agencies' relationship with the concept of liability has always been dependent upon its environment. The environment that surrounded the early reporting agencies, one defined by relatively primitive trading standards and technologies, was essentially an SME-focused affair. The 'businesses' the mercantile agencies usually focused upon were smaller businesses (though they rated all types of businesses, of course). Yet, for the early credit rating agencies, things were different. They were not only rating companies, but actively rating the securities that those companies were providing for invest-ment. That, conceptually, is very different from what the mercantile agencies were concerned with (though connected). From the perspective of liability, this raises very different questions. For example, whereas libel and slander were the liability-related issues that the mercantile agencies focused on predominantly, for the credit rating agencies those same issues tended to be less important on the face of things. Securities had owners, and companies had boards, whilst the SMEs the mercantile agencies were focused on were often family-run businesses or the sole concern of singular business owners. Therefore, the liability landscape had changed.

The effect of this is that we should start now asking different questions at this stage of the book. Automatically, the changing complexities facing the credit rating agencies mean that the issues of liability quickly became more systemic in nature. Mistakes or inaccuracies with the early mercantile agencies resulted in issues with individual business owners, whereas mistakes or inaccuracies with the credit rating agencies could quickly cause financial crises. However, this understanding is based upon a foundation that we have today that did not exist for the early credit rating agencies. Today, as we shall learn later in the chapter, there is an undercurrent of systemic reliance in relation to the utility of the credit rating industry because of repeated instances of regulators and legislators utilising the ratings to achieve systemic objectives. In the early 1900s, there was no such systemic interference within the (American) financial sector. Arguably, this is why the American economy was so unstable and volatile, and why initiatives like the Federal Reserve were established. That regulatory 'gap', as it were, was closed as the country began to reel from the sheer volume of economic crises in the 1920s and 1930s.

There are two prevailing streams of thought on the developments for the credit rating agencies in the 1930s, one more 'mainstream' than the other. The first suggests that the 1930s marked the first stage of two stages that laid the groundwork for what became the GFC in 2007/08. According to the 'regulatory licence' school of thought, the actions of regulators in the 1930s fundamentally forced the ratings of the early rating industry onto the marketplace and began what would come to be known as 'regulatory reliance'. As Partnoy says:

> ...the regulatory licence view helps explain the increase in the importance of credit rating agencies during the 1930s and from the mid-1970s through today. According to this view, ratings are valuable, not because they are accurate and credible, but because they are the key to reducing costs associated with regulation, which increased during the mentioned periods. In theory, rating agencies have good reason to avoid conflicts of interest and to protect the accuracy of their ratings, because they need to preserve their reputations. However, once the ratings of a small number of credit rating agencies are enshrined by regulators who incorporate credit ratings into substantive regulation, the markets become less vigilant about the agencies' work.[18]

This challenge to the 'reputational capital' sentiment, which suggests that rating agencies will be hesitant to take decisions which could threaten their reputation in the eyes of investors, has proven to be a dominant theory for explaining the performance of credit rating agencies in the recent past. Whilst rating agency officials are keen to remind the market that without their reputation they would not be able to operate, the broad consensus is that the pressure that reputational damage can bring is very much on the decline, if not totally irrelevant.[19] Whether or not the perceived forcing of the ratings onto the marketplace by regulators is the cause of that is up for debate, but that is the 'mainstream' viewpoint on the matter.

The core of these beliefs comes in two parts: the first based in the 1930s, and the second in the 1970s. In the 1930s, regulatory reliance-focused scholars have used the actions of certain regulators as the evidence for the systematic incorporating of the ratings, and then have evaluated the effects of the regulatory strategies. Partnoy suggests that, in the 1920s, the credit rating agencies were only used in very limited circumstances and had very little utility.[20] Then, apparently without much warning or rationale, major regulators began incorporating the credit ratings into their mandates. For example, whilst Federal Reserve Banks began utilising the ratings in their examinations of things like banking portfolios and calculating capital requirements, the Comptroller of the Currency, in 1931, directly adopted the rule that credit ratings were to become proper measures of the quality of national banks' bond accounts; specifically 'the Comptroller ruled that bonds rated BBB (or the equivalent rating) or higher could be carried at cost, but bonds with lower ratings (including defaulted bonds) required fractional write-offs'.[21] Furthermore, certain investments by savings banks and trust funds were deemed 'legal' based upon ratings, leading to the terminology of 'legals' being used to describe what could be purchased and what could not – equivalent to what we have today with certain institutions (systemically important ones like pension funds) being unable to invest in bonds that are not deemed to be of 'investment grade'. Partnoy provides accounts that suggest that, overnight, more than 1,000 bonds instantly failed to meet the new thresholds, resulting in chaos and protest from market participants.

Nevertheless, Partnoy argues that this inclusion of credit ratings into the financial regulatory architecture did not instantly result in a dramatic raising of the agencies' fortunes. Even though other regulators continued the trend of incorporating the ratings into their practices and rulings (like in relation to the insurance industry, as just one example),[22] Partnoy tells us that from the end of the 1930s up until the 1960s, the credit rating agencies were contracting, not expanding. Furthermore, in the 1960s, the agencies were apparently facing 'extinction', employing only half a dozen analysts each. The fact that Moody's was purchased and subsumed into the Dun & Bradstreet Corporation in 1962, and S&P was purchased by McGraw-Hill four years later, perhaps supports this view. Instead of the 1930s being the era that incorporated the credit rating agencies into the fibre of the economy, Partnoy argues that the actions of the SEC in the 1970s were the truly inclusive era for credit ratings, with the adoption of Rule 15c3-1 in 1975 becoming the first securities rule in US history to formally incorporate the credit rating agencies themselves, as opposed to just their ratings. It was this rule that brought about the designation of 'Nationally Registered Statistical Rating Organisation', or NRSRO as it is more commonly known. This regulatory designation, which was then incorporated into a wide variety of rules and regulations across the board, is the prime example cited by the 'regulatory licence' school of thought. The point here is that 'regulation has created a captive demand for ratings'[23] which, as a dynamic, 'deprives investors of their most effective – if not only – weapon to prevent dishonest ratings and encourage accuracy: the ability to retaliate, by not trusting ratings anymore'.[24]

There are, as I have shown elsewhere, a multitude of challenges to this school of thought, particularly in relation to the understanding of the chain of events leading up to the SEC's decisions in the 1970s (which we will cover shortly). However, Flandreau and his colleagues have produced a body of work that takes a wider view still.[25] Instead of just focusing on the rating agencies, Flandreau makes the connection between the reporting agencies and the rating agencies and examines their relationship with authority in a constant manner. What this wider lens does is allow for very different analyses to be undertaken and very different questions that can be put forward. One such question, given the wider lens, is whether such a holistic view can answer for us the foundational question of why rating/reporting agencies became so useful, or at least utilised?

Instead of focusing on the role of the regulator, Flandreau and his colleagues instead focus on the systemic role of the provider of reports/ratings. Starting with the early mercantile agencies, Flandreau and Mesevage suggest that 'what mercantile agencies achieved ("invented") was a form of the separation of information and lending – a "commoditisation of credit information"'.[26] Interestingly, Flandreau et al. endeavour to show that instead of a regulatory licence being the dominant mode of operation, systemically, that licence was actually foreshadowed by a 'legal licence' provided for by the judiciary. The implication therefore is that instead of forcing the early credit rating agencies onto an unsuspecting marketplace, the evolution from reporting to rating agency was not a surprise to the marketplace (in fact, it was something they wanted/needed) and, when the Comptroller in the 1930s sought to install the ratings of the agencies into regulation and practice, it was done without much associated supporting materials; the marketplace did not need support in understanding what the credit rating agencies and their ratings were, as they were already widely using them.

Yet, the concept of a 'legal licence' suggests the support of the legal system for the reports developed by the mercantile agencies, and also their effect. Upon inspection, Flandreau et al. find that this is far from the case. Rather, between 1880 and 1900, research found that R.G. Dun & Co., the leading mercantile agency after Robert Dun had purchased the Mercantile Agency from the remnants of Lewis Tappan's efforts, was sued for libel in more than 100 cases. The issue at hand was whether the reports qualified as 'qualified privilege', a term used to describe the instance where a provider of information was granted an exception to libel law if they were providing socially useful information.[27] Rather than provide this legal support, the courts often found against the reporting agency *when it had the chance to do so*. Yet, that was not very often at all because, as Flandreau et al. found, many suits did not make it all the way because of a variety of strategies employed by the agencies, including intimidation, legal delay, and chicanery, and mostly utilising their established power against weaker litigants. Where the courts did positively cite reporting agencies and early rating agencies, they did so in *acknowledgement* of commercial practice by entities such as banks, rather than acknowledging the benefits or otherwise of the ratings/reports themselves.

This leads Flandreau to suggest that instead of regulators in the 1930s forcing the ratings onto the market, there was instead a 'seamless transition between court arbitration and regulatory arrangements'.[28] One of the most important effects of this understanding is that the courts and the regulators were *reacting* to market practice, which, potentially, shines a new light on the foundational question I asked above regarding the usefulness or utility of the act of rating/reporting. Usefully, as Flandreau and Mesevage discuss, the reality is that the act of commercialising credit analysis gave rise to a form of *private order* in providing protection to investors/lenders that was provided for in other jurisdictions by law. Speaking of the early mercantile agencies, the scholars say that 'as godfathers of US capitalism, Bradstreet and R.G. Dun could be alternately and aptly described as... benevolent providers of that order'. The bourgeoning America had produced a private problem, and the private sector provided its own solution.

What does this understanding tell us in relation to the concept of liability? To begin with, it puts the concept of regulating or legislating a rating sector into a new, perhaps much more understanding, light. We shall uncover more of this systemic characteristic of the rating concept throughout this book, but if the act of rating is so systemically important to the functioning of capitalism, how does one regulate that act? How can one constrain the actions of the agencies, perhaps in trying to stop them from monetising their centralised position too much, when the provision of their product is so critical? Furthermore, the actual dynamics of what the system requires only increased the acute pressure placed upon those tasked with regulating such industries.

As a short aside before moving on, those dynamics are worth focusing on. You may be wondering how rating agencies have become so powerful, even though their products are considered so critically important. It is because of the *way* in which those products are required that leads to a deeper understanding. The concept of monopoly is widely known, as is the multiple-based version of an *oligopoly*, meaning a market of many sellers. However, in the credit rating market, just like the credit reporting market before it, there is clear evidence that only a few select providers are favoured and that this select group does not change. For example, the Mercantile Agency, which turned into R.G. Dun & Co., was met with competition from John Bradstreet's eponymously named company, and that is it. After some initial market reorganising, the credit rating industry settled into Moody's, the merger between Standard Statistics and Henry Poor's company in the 1940s, and to a much lesser extent John Fitch's company later on, and that is it. It has been suggested that these patterns have emerged because the rating oligopoly is what is known as a *natural oligopoly*.

The concept of an oligopoly being a natural one was skilfully dissected by Shaked and Sutton in the 1980s,[29] but in relation to the credit rating industry, the work of Schroeter is extremely useful.[30] We shall see later in the chapter that regulatory effort after regulatory effort in the credit rating space, particularly surrounding the GFC and afterwards, failed. If we join this to the understanding above that the core systemic function of a rating makes regulating the agencies who produce them extraordinarily difficult, the result is that it does not matter what a regulator or legislator does, 'the market dominance of Moody's, Standard & Poor's, and Fitch [will remain] completely unaffected'. There have been theoretical arguments put forward, which have been adopted by regulators somewhat unwisely, that suggest that there are barriers to entry, like in the form of competition, which need to be brought down to instil more discipline into the sector. This, in effect, is the outcome of the 'regulatory licence' argument in a sense. However, counter-theories have argued that the reality is that:

> a natural oligopoly is a market structure in which a small number of firms compete, and natural or legal barriers restrict the entry of new firms. The prevailing theoretical explanation of the rating oligopoly assumes that new competitors cannot enter the market because they lack features necessary to gain acceptance for their ratings (like the sufficient track record or governmental recognition), suggesting that the barriers to entry reside on the supply-side of the market.[31]

Yet, as Schroeter discusses, this does not explain how the 'Big Three' have been the dominant force throughout the history of the credit rating agencies, with their market share being almost unmoved over decades of existence. To answer that element, Schroeter argues that:

> The evidence suggests that the decisive barrier to entry rather resides on the rating market's demand-side, namely the investors' preference for a market with only a few rating suppliers: Since a central reason for credit ratings' usefulness to

investors is that they reduce complexity by distilling a wealth of market information into an easy-to-process rating symbol, this advantage would be lost again, had the investors to assimilate and process ratings from a large number of competing credit rating agencies. Financial markets frequented by investors with a limited capacity to assimilate and process information – the latter being a natural characteristic of real-world investors, although not reflected in the theoretical economic model of an efficient market – therefore always result in an investor-driven natural oligopoly of rating suppliers, making attempts to increase the number of relevant credit rating agencies futile.[32]

It is therefore important to constantly remember the real dynamics at play in the credit rating space. The actual usefulness of the ratings the agencies produce has long since been called into question,[33] which then brings forward several considerations. One consideration is that if the ratings that are widely and systemically used are not that useful, then why are they used? Perhaps it is the answer to that question that will make sense of the naturalness of the rating oligopoly?

I argue strongly that this is the case. The answer to why credit ratings are systemically used despite having their usefulness in question is, I argue, because they serve a systemic purpose far more important than direct usefulness. I have argued elsewhere that it is the application of *signalling theory* that provides all the answers that we need.[34] The application of signalling theory tells us that the genius of the credit rating is that it, at once, codifies incredibly sensitive information, resolves the asymmetrical problem by way of injecting perceived third-party independence, and displays an output which is painfully simple in its understanding: it does not take great intelligence to understand that AAA is higher than C. However, if this is the case, then how does a natural oligopoly fit into this understanding? Well, if the aim is to *signal* your position, i.e., your creditworthiness, to a variety of prospective investors, having too many vehicles to carry that signal will cause duplicative costs for the signaller, and distort the signal for the receiver. The oligopoly is not natural because the agencies want it that way; it is natural because the market wants it that way. Too many chefs will certainly spoil the broth.

If we accept this, then things that may have confused previously start to make sense. The judiciary and regulators were reacting to what the market needed, and they could do nothing else; otherwise they would have negatively affected the flow of capital. The NRSRO designation is merely a footprint because, in reality, the marketplace had designated those who it would use, and nothing else could penetrate that group of rating agencies. Furthermore, in the case of applying liability, credit reporting agencies and credit rating agencies have a natural defence, in that their products are *required*. We shall see as we continue with the chapter that the agencies know this reality and use it to their advantage, as one would expect them to do. As we progress into the rest of the chapter, I will return to this concept again and again in order to properly contextualise actions and decisions that may seem strange without the necessary context.

4.   THE LIABILITY LITMUS TEST FOR CREDIT RATING AGENCIES

The question of applying liability to the credit rating space is a nuanced one. The reality is that there are underlying forces at play which fundamentally determine whether one can even apply liability to the credit rating agencies, and then how impactful that liability may be in terms of deterrence and/or wealth restoration. Whilst this book is not a historical book, it is worth continuing our journey through the different stages of the sector's development because key characteristics were developed in earlier stages that would go on to affect the ability to apply liability within the sector.

The 1960s and 1970s is a good place to start. We heard in the last section that the SEC, via its Rule 15c3-1 in 1973–75, essentially enshrined the leading rating agencies with their NRSRO designation, with the effect being to ringfence the agencies and force reliance from the marketplace upon them. Leaving aside the challenge to that theory for a moment, the actual thought process of the SEC deserves attention because, if we take it at face value that they actually did ringfence the leading agencies, then the effect of this in terms of applying liability should be obvious: how can you apply liability to something you force onto the market?

As usual, the reality is somewhat different from that common understanding. Perhaps the prime example of this is the Penn Central collapse in 1970. The collapsing of one of the largest railroad companies in the US at the time provides illustration for both the understanding that the provision of *ratings*, conceptually, is systemically important but also that narratives can be misleading. The dominant narrative that plays into the reputational capital/regulatory licence schools of thought is that:

> During the Vietnam War, bond price volatility increased somewhat, as did issuance of commercial paper, and borrowers faced a severe credit contraction. Demand for credit information increased during this period, but the agencies remained relatively small and not obviously important as a source of information to issuers or investors. At the time, the rating agencies employed only a few analysts each and generated revenues primarily from the sale of published research reports. The market did not place great value on those research reports, presumably, according to the reputational capital view, because rating agencies had lost a large portion of their reputational capital. Moreover, as the commercial paper market expanded rapidly during the 1960s, investors were not very precise in assessing credit quality. In the fallout of the 1970 Penn Central default on $82 million of commercial paper, investors began demanding more sophisticated levels of research. The rating agencies, still

relatively small and without substantial reputational capital, were not in a position to satisfy this demand.[35]

The sentiment here, in relation to the regulatory licence theory, is that the SEC's rule in 1975 essentially provided the rating agencies to satisfy this market-based demand. A similar misunderstanding comes in relation to the commercial paper market, which is a form of short-term financing. Hudson et al. said of the pre-1970s environment for commercial paper investment that prior to the collapsing of Penn Central, which collapsed with $82 million of commercial paper outstanding, 'investors relied on name recognition as the principal criterion for issuer selection'.[36] However, a closer inspection into the time shows a very different environment and one that perhaps single-handedly shows why a natural oligopoly must always exist when it comes to assessing creditworthiness in the open marketplace.

Rather than investors relying mainly on 'name recognition' – which, as a concept in and of itself is a remarkable one given that millions and millions of dollars would therefore have been invested upon something so transient and unreliable – another re-examination of the credit rating genealogy reveals the reasoning behind the development of the commercial paper market. As part of the merger between R.G. Dun & Co. and the Bradstreet Company in 1933, Dun positioned a man named Arthur D. Whiteside at the helm of the company, in the role of CEO. As part of this amalgamation, Whiteside brought with him his own endeavour, the National Credit Office, which he had used to change the approach of the reporting business from providing products to providing 'service'. In the following years, and into the 1960s where Dun & Bradstreet would purchase the stricken Moody's, the National Credit Office (NCO) would become the home of the group's *commercial paper* ratings, with their top rating being the so-called 'Prime' rating, akin to today's AAA rating.

As the market grew in the 1960s for short-term lending, there were two competing factors in contributing to the financial crisis that ensued in the early 1970s. The first is that the dominant market leader in selling commercial paper securities was Goldman Sachs, who with its 'name recognition' also confirmed to its prospective customers that 'it only offered paper rated "prime" by NCO, an independent credit rating service'.[37] This was purposefully included in marketing materials because a number of prospective investors in commercial paper were obliged by regulation to only invest in securities highly rated by a rating entity and, lest we forget, before 1975 there was no official ringfenced group of who that may be. In fact, in relation to commercial paper ratings, the NCO was the *only* rating entity producing commercial paper ratings at that time, meaning there was essentially a rating monopoly in that specific and growing marketplace.

In scenes reminiscent of the GFC that would come nearly 40 years later, the combination of investors forced to utilise a monopolistic rating process, and a rating industry closely aligned to the sellers of securities rather than the investors (NCO and Goldman Sachs actively worked on commercial paper deals together and collaborated in various other guises, unbeknownst to the investors) had the obvious result of a massive systemic failure. Congressional investigations into the financial crisis that ensued from the then-largest financial crash in modern history when Penn Central unexpectedly collapsed were unequivocal in prescribing blame for the crisis. They declared that the NCO has directly 'contributed to the misleading of investors'. They also found that of the 651 outstanding NCO ratings at the time of the Penn Central collapse, all but 34 still carried the 'Prime' rating, indicating widescale rating inflation. Furthermore, the ratings were found to be very poorly maintained, if at all, and also there was direct collaboration between the analysts and executives in charge at the NCO, and Goldman Sachs in advance of investors finding out about the deteriorating situation at Penn Central.[38] To further accentuate this point, post-GFC court cases where investors were seeking to recover lost resources found, across the board, that the NCO 'had no idea of the underlying risk to the issuances they were rating'.[39]

The details of the collapse and the role of the NCO have been chronicled elsewhere,[40] but its relationship to our analysis will now become clear, if it was not already. Whilst the NCO and Dun & Bradstreet would be publicly vilified for their role in the crisis, the rating agencies had downgraded Penn Central relatively early and had managed to stay out of the firing line because of a lack of connection to the commercial paper market. At the same time, technological advancements were threatening the livelihood of the rating agencies; the public sale of photocopying machines[41] meant that rating agencies were no longer able to protect their intellectual property (ratings) and they were directly exposed to the phenomenon of 'free riding', where investors can freely duplicate the ratings they purchase. Hopefully you can see here the aligning of the stars for the credit rating agencies – and it is a picture that is very different from the 'SEC forced the ratings onto the market' picture. Issuers of debt, in needing to signal their quality to a recently harmed investing public, needed a clean third party with which to do so, and the facilitative NCO was no longer a viable option. Into that void stepped the credit rating agencies, and crucially they had developed a plan for resolving their free-riding problem: they would charge issuers for ratings, instead of investors. They started with municipal borrowers, and quickly expanded it across all issuer classes. Moody's would take the lead in charging corporate issuers, and Standard & Poor's would follow suit four years later in 1973. In 1973, the SEC promulgated its new rule and the NRSRO ringfence was effectively constructed.

There are lessons to be learned here before we move on. The revelation that research has found direct evidence that shows rating inflation increasing once the credit rating agencies began charging issuers should not come as a surprise,[42] but what is key for us is the understanding that no matter the cost, the informational asymmetry problem *must* be resolved for the marketplace. The clear reputational damage done to the concept of 'rating' by the performance of the NCO is almost irrelevant because, whilst the NCO would not survive the post-GFC attacks, the credit rating agencies, one of whom operated under the very same parent as the NCO (Moody's was also under Dun & Bradstreet), could quickly utilise the crisis to not only prosper, but fully change their remuneration model whereby now they were directly inserting the very same conflict that blighted the NCO. To the marketplace, it mattered little. Investors needed to say they were investing in products that had been considered by a theoretically reputable and independent third party, and as long as those requirements were met, the marketplace was relatively happy. Schroeter's earlier pronouncement that the naturalness of the rating oligopoly was investor-driven appears to be the truest sentiment ever written about the rating space.

Yet, if it is investor-driven, the implications for applying liability in the space are stark. The concept of *reliance* in a legal sense then comes into play, and it is an extraordinarily subjective and difficult-to-define concept in the real world, as Lehmann explains:

> While one can easily justify compensation awarded to an issuer that was improperly rated by a CRA under ordinary principles of tort law, similar justification is not so readily available for the claim of an investor who has suffered damage caused by an incorrect rating. An investor is not obliged to rely on the rating. Moreover, he typically does not pay for it. Under the current 'issuer-pays model', he receives his information for free since it is the issuer who pays the agency to acquire a rating. The liability that arises under the CRA regulation therefore seems like a gratis guarantee for the investor. He can effectively shift the risk inherent in his investment decisions over to the rating agencies without incurring any direct cost.[43]

This moral hazard has, since the rating agencies transformed their remuneration models, been at the heart of the liability questions applied to the industry. As we shall see shortly, the effect of providing the investors with a 'gratis guarantee' would arguably have systemic effects witnessed in the GFC.

The GFC of 2007/08, underpinned by toxic residential-backed mortgage securities (RMBS), is the current generation's Wall Street Crash of 1929 and sparked a similarly impactful economic downturn afterwards. The societal effects of the GFC have yet to be fully played out, but the causes of the GFC were years in the making. Post-GFC Congressional investigations have aptly chronicled the major causes of the GFC,[44] whilst there have also been libraries of books developed on the subject since.[45] It is therefore not overly necessary to detail every angle of the lead-up to the GFC, but some stand-out aspects are worthy of consideration. As we are looking at liability in the rating space, the particular and granular targets for the exposure to liability have their roots in the particular developments that were established years before the GFC. For instance, the complexity involved in the sale of RMBS products meant that credit rating agencies were integral to resolving the inherent informational asymmetry at play, but also that there were only certain investors who could partake in the marketplace. You may have noticed that this is almost identical to the Penn Central collapse. That duality has implications, however.

Explained in a very simple manner, an RMBS product contains the pooling of many residential mortgage products into one 'stream' of payments. The role of the rating agencies was (a) to understand the underlying risk once all of the mortgages were pooled together, and (b) to then siphon that 'stream' of revenue to the appropriate level of investor depending upon their risk appetite. This complex method of finance is known as developing 'tranches' (the French word for slice) and the ratings of the agencies would determine the likelihood of repayment by tranche. So, the highest tranche would be rated AAA, for example, and those investors partaking in the investment within the top tranche would be almost guaranteed to receive a full return on their investment, and on time. Furthermore, the tranche approach was sold to investors in a cascading manner, so that those higher in the waterfall would be more protected from losses. The higher tranches would see investment from systemically important investors like pension funds who, coincidentally, were only allowed to invest in products rated AAA. At the bottom end were hedge funds and the like, who were almost unregulated, chased higher returns, and had a much more substantial risk appetite; they would feel the losses first if the mortgages in the pool started to default.

Yet, the above is merely the theory of the process. The real-world implementation of the process was very different. Post-GFC investigations pointed the finger in various directions. One proposed culprit was the American mortgage institutions called Fannie Mae and Freddie Mac, who critics proposed were artificially inflating the mortgage market by incentivising new mortgage deals via purchasing agreements on a systemic level.[46] Others pointed to inherent faults within the private mortgage origination marketplace, with the enhanced requirement to find purchasers of mortgage deals, stemming from pressure from RMBS originators like investment banks, leading to an array of wholly inappropriate practices. Practices like the falsification of records, and pushing so-called NINJA loans – for people deemed to have 'No Income, No Job, No Assets' – were commonplace in the lead-up to the pinnacle of the GFC. Finally, the credit rating agencies were held as centrally accountable as key gatekeepers because post-GFC investigation found that the rating agencies were guilty of several failures. The first was that they generally had no real idea of the underlying riskiness of the mortgages within the pools they were rating. The rating agencies responded by saying that their role is not to verify the underlying assets, but merely assess them, and if records were being fraudulently falsified, that is a data problem, not an analytical problem. There is merit in this argument, but only ever so slightly. The reality is that a fraction of the mortgages put into RMBS products were fraudulently developed. Second, the credit rating agencies were alleged to have heavily inflated their ratings for inflated fees from a handful of powerful and centrally positioned investment banks, just like the NCO did in the Penn Central collapse with Goldman Sachs. Third, the rating agencies were alleged to have actively worked with investment banks to design products that would garner the desired ratings for the banks to then sell them to investors. This, again, is directly relatable to the Penn Central collapse.

There are key notions in relation to the allegations levied against the credit rating agencies. Not only were they alleged to have acted against the investors who they articulate they serve (despite being paid by the issuer), but the whole RMBS system had unique characteristics that are vital to understand when we look at it all with a liability-focused lens. The RMBS market was not an open one, and a lot of the RMBS products were placed into special 'vehicles', mainly to constrain the liability for all involved. The investment banks and credit rating agencies actively designed those 'vehicles' so that they could meet the requirements of the different categories of investors, whilst also allowing the credit rating agencies to apportion their top ratings which were necessary for the products to be sold. Crucially, only 'qualified' investors were usually allowed to partake in the purchasing of slices of the RMBS via those vehicles. The implication with regards to liability exposure for the credit rating agencies was that they would have known, precisely, who the investors were before partaking in the design of the product and also afterwards when maintenance should have been front and centre. This understanding alone focuses the liability parameters because one of the key defences for the credit rating agencies is the so-called 'floodgates' defence, which describes the notion of the rating agencies (or any entity) being exposed to so much liability that any opening of the gate would devour their business. Also, the credit rating agencies have traditionally had one key defence, and that is that their ratings constitute mere 'opinions' which should not be relied upon. The vehicular mode of operating within the RMBS process means that, technically, the investors *had* to rely on the ratings assigned to the different RMBS products.

These underlying dynamics provided the backdrop for what would be the first systematic attempt to apply liability to the credit rating agencies. Their actions had been proven, and the fervour for action after the height of the GFC was enough to warrant intensive action. In the US, the host of the GFC, and the EU – who would just be about to find themselves thrust into the heat of the GFC and see their very existence threatened – the credit rating agencies were on the chopping block. Both jurisdictions attempted to apply liability to the rating agencies in their own way. However, as we shall see in the next section, the methods to apply that liability and the success with which they did so varied dramatically.

5. APPLYING SYSTEMATIC LIABILITY FOR THE FIRST TIME

There was an Act of Congress in the US directed at the credit rating agencies before the GFC, although it came far too late and was made almost immediately irrelevant. The Credit Rating Agency Reform Act of 2006 sought to insert more accountability into rating procedures, give the SEC more authority in its role as overseer of the industry, increase competition by inducing smaller agencies into the NRSRO designation, and essentially inject some rudimentary base standards (the likes of which the rating agencies would have been doing anyway).[47] Prior to the GFC, the European Union had never sought to regulate the activities of the rating agencies. In the Credit Rating Agency Reform Act of 2006, the words 'liability' or 'liable' was only mentioned once in something unconnected to rating agency liability. That was the pre-GFC environment for rating agency liability.

However, all that would swiftly change. The European Union was first to act, acknowledging that the credit rating agencies were mostly headquartered outside of the European Community and national laws rarely dealt with the rating agencies. The first of what would be three distinct regulations was enacted in 2009 and aimed to establish a common framework of credit rating-related rules across the Community. Those rules ranged from minimum standards, the start of what would become methodological transparency, and other base-level rulings. In terms of liability, the word was only used four times and made it clear that 'any claim against credit rating agencies in relation to any infringement of the provisions of this Regulation should be made in accordance with the applicable national law on civil liability'.[48] The uncomplicated understanding of this pronouncement is that the European Commission refused to make liability in the credit rating space a continental endeavour and thought that the civil liability regimes within member states' legal frameworks would be enough to provide routes to resolve harm caused by the agencies. Lehmann suggests that this tactic was a purposeful one, taking into account political difficulties in the multi-state bloc:

> We may in fact witness here a new strategy. Referring the details of a regulation to Member States is in fact a very convenient way to mask political disagreement.

European Parliamentarians were able to endorse the draft independently of whether they liked rating agency liability or not. In times when the public does not stop complaining about too much intrusion and over-regulation by the EU, it must have seemed very sensible for them to transfer some responsibility back to the Member States. At the same time, they avoided the risk of their constituencies reproaching them that the European Parliament would not have acted against rating agencies. The governments represented in the Council were happy to follow the path shown to them by the Parliament. There was something in the new draft for everybody. Those governments that wanted some visible action against rating agencies could point to the fact that liability was introduced. And those who secretly nurtured doubts about the wisdom of such liability could take comfort in the thought that they would still have an opportunity on the national level to determine how far such liability actually went. The resulting compromise is very strange indeed. We now have an EU cause of action on the books. But to know whether a rating agency is liable, one will have to look to Member State law. Empty lawmaking has never been done more artfully. But there is no reason for the EU bodies to congratulate themselves. Their latest trick may backfire once the public becomes fully aware that the Regulation is for the Member States just the staging of a new version of 'As you like it'. It also does not help the industry, which would probably have preferred a uniform regime because it offers legal certainty. Far from having strengthened the EU, the new version of the CRA Regulation may endanger its importance and its credibility as a lawmaker.[49]

This 'empty law-making', as Lehmann calls it, proved to be short-lived. The need to properly account for the potential harm that could be done by the credit rating agencies was turning palpable in the European Union and events just two years later would bring the credit rating problem straight to the door of the European Union.

In the US, just a year after the EU first took action, Congress enacted its response to the GFC. The Act's long title was 'An Act to promote the financial stability of the United States by improving accountability and transparency in the financial system, to end "too big to fail", to protect the American taxpayer by ending bailouts, to protect consumers from abusive financial services practices, and for other purposes'. Known more colloquially by its shortened title 'The Dodd-Frank Act of 2010' after its congressional sponsors, the Act was unsurprisingly wide-ranging. It covered a variety of industries, from banking to credit rating, and established a variety of new regulatory bodies and re-evaluated the authority of existing regulators. Within Title IX, subtitle C, the Act covered the credit rating industry and presented solid and extensive reforms for the first time, very much eclipsing the 2006 Act.

The section of the Act had several aims. It took aim at the regulation, accountability, and transparency associated with the industry, as well as seeking to fully remove reference to the ratings of the agencies within federal statute. It also set up the Office for Credit Ratings within the SEC as a designated regulatory focal point for regulating credit rating activities, as well as insisting on base standards in the areas of analyst training (for the first time) and aspects such as the timing of ratings and the comparability of rating symbols (and the visibility of them). However, perhaps the main focus and arguably the most contentious was the decision to openly expose the credit rating agencies to liability for the first time, bringing them in line with other financial analysis-focused industries. As Hemraj explains:

> Historically, the *Securities Act 1933* considered CRAs as experts since ratings are inherently forward looking and embody assumptions and predictions about future events that by their nature cannot be verified as facts. The new law rescinds Rule 436(g), thus exposing CRAs to expert liability if they consent to be named in registration statements and related prospectuses. Under Dodd-Frank, there is a lower pleading requirement for claimants' lawsuits, both in the government and private, against CRAs. Dodd-Frank also modifies the ability of CRAs [credit rating agencies] to receive certain information of a material, non-public nature from issuers.[50]

The Act had changed the very nature of providing ratings in the United States, exposing the agencies to more liability overnight than they had been throughout their history.

However, whilst that details the congressional will in 2010, the larger and historic picture of applying liability in the rating space is very different indeed. Picciau discusses how 'despite the most recent regulatory interventions, major obstacles still remain to establishing liability for inaccurate ratings in the United States, the main being perhaps the First Amendment to the US Constitution'.[51] She continues by explaining for us that the First Amendment was first invoked in the *Jaillet v. Cashman* case in 1921 concerning real-time stock exchange information and its dissemination but, as Partnoy illustrates, the judiciary have never settled on a position regarding credit rating liability whenever a case did manage to find its way into a courtroom:

> Rating agencies were sued following a number of defaults, including class action litigation related to the Washington Public Power Supply System default in 1983; claims related to the Executive Life bankruptcy in 1991; a suit by the Jefferson County, Colorado, School District against Moody's in 1995; and claims by Orange County, California, based on professional negligence, against S&P in 1996. However, the only common element in these cases was that the rating agencies won. The suits were dismissed or settled on favorable terms to the rating agencies. For example, Orange County's $2 billion suit against S&P nettled a paltry settlement of $140,000, roughly 0.007 percent of the claimed damages. A more recent example was the portion of the consolidated Enron litigation involving claims brought by the Connecticut Resources Recovery Authority. Consider the following statement from the Houston federal district court hearing that case: 'After reviewing the case law regarding credit rating agencies and a number of reports and law review articles, this Court finds that generally the courts have not held credit rating agencies accountable for alleged professional negligence or fraud and that plaintiffs have not prevailed in litigation against them. Moreover, there is even a statutory exemption under the Securities Act of 1933 for Section 11 claims against credit rating agencies like the

three Defendants here that have been designated "nationally recognized statistical rating agencies" or "NRSROs."'

The Enron court, like some other courts, extended a qualified First Amendment protection to credit rating agencies.[52]

However, in perhaps illustrating the evolving nature of the case law in the area, 2003 saw a case be heard that provided a new insight into what was possible when applying liability. Crucially, in *Re Fitch* in 2003, the Court of Appeal for the Second Circuit:

> provided an innovative interpretation of the law, according to which in case of solicited ratings, when the rating organisation is significantly involved in the client's transactions (as it typically happens for structured products), the agencies cannot be treated as journalists, with obvious consequences on the applicability of the First Amendment.[53]

This legal development is best understood in the context of a larger legal trend in relation to 'professional negligence' and the associated 'duty of care' that professionals have to their clientele or the wider public at large if in such a position. In the rating space, as Picciau helpfully explains, the opportunity to apply liability usually revolves around the concept of 'negligent misrepresentation' and, in order to argue for negligent misrepresentation, the claimant must establish a duty of care which requires the claimant to also show that they were in 'privity' with the defendant (the rating agency). Privity describes when there is a substantive legal relationship between two or more parties and, in the rating space, this can develop:

> if the agency knows the identity of the limited group of recipients of the credit rating or, according to a different approach, if the judgement is distributed to, or reserved to the use of, a limited number of recipients and not the public at large, regardless of whether the professional knows the recipients' identity.[54]

This facet was also confirmed in *LaSalle v. Duff & Phelps* in the 1990s.[55]

Cutting through this legalese, the sentiment here relates back to the conversation earlier in the chapter regarding 'floodgates' and the application of liability. The courts have mostly made clear that if the rating agency is providing ratings just generally, and for wide and potentially unlimited use, then liability will not be imposed. But, if the agency is either helping to construct products or knows (a) the specific identity of those using the ratings or (b) knows that only a select group of investors will ever be using the ratings, then the door for liability will be opened. The decision to move the law into this pathway in 2003 was a warning for credit rating agencies but, at that point, they had already committed to performing acts that would see them held up as central players in the degeneration of standards across the financial sector; it was too late to turn the massive ship around.

To add further complexity to this picture, the Dodd-Frank Act said, in sub-section 933:

> In the case of an action for money damages brought against a credit rating agency or a controlling person under this title, it shall be sufficient, for purposes of pleading any required state of mind in relation to such action, that the complaint state with particularity facts giving rise to a strong inference that the credit rating agency knowingly or recklessly failed—(i) to conduct a reasonable investigation of the rated security with respect to the factual elements relied upon by its own methodol-ogy for evaluating credit risk; or (ii) to obtain reasonable verification of such factual elements (which verification may be based on a sampling technique that does not amount to an audit) from other sources that the credit rating agency considered to be competent and that were independent of the issuer and underwriter.

This is problematic for a variety of reasons. Chief amongst them all is the requirement for the claimant to 'state with particularity' facts show the credit rating agency failed to conduct a reasonable investigation of the security in relation to its stated methodologies. In extrapolating from this, the onus is on the claimant to show, definitively, when a rating agency was *consciously* acting against the position of the claimant. Now, if the rating world is new to you, I can confirm for you that it is a particularly shadowy, closed world. Obtaining such information is nigh-on impossible and, with the oligopolistic makeup of the upper echelons of the credit rating space, finding information from within the closed circle seems to be an exceptionally prohibitive barrier.

So, in the US, this high bar is the first major issue. The second is the ruling in the Dodd-Frank Act that removes the protections of being exempt from Section 11 liability (bringing the agencies in line with other financial analysts and auditors). Section 11 only applies to experts 'if they consent to have their expert opinions be part of the registration statement'.[56] To the eagle-eyed amongst you there is a very clear 'out' in that statement that the rating agencies could take and, in mid-2010, the rating agencies did exactly that. The first time the SEC had the chance to deal with this issue was when Ford Motor Company's finance arm raised the point that, under Regulation AB in the US, an issuer of an asset-backed security (ABS) must attach to the registration document the rating of one or more credit rating agency. Exposed to such exposure after the exemption to Section 11 liability was removed, the credit rating agencies simply informed Ford that they would not consent to having their rating attached to the registration document (prospectus) and, effectively, stopped the issuance from going ahead. The move and its implications were amplified for every other issuer of asset-backed securities, with the implication being that the ABS market would be *completely* shut down, causing financial catastrophe. Instantly, the SEC stepped in and sent a 'no-action letter' to Ford, saying that they would not take enforcement action under Regulation AB if they were to market ABS without the rating of an agency attached.[57] The result was to allow ABS to be sold again, but the associated result was that Section 11 liability was *immediately* removed from the equation because you cannot apply liability to a credit rating agency that does not have its rating attached to the financial product. More than 13 years later, campaigners are still requesting that the SEC pulls this letter to instil liability again in the marketplace,[58] all to no avail: the risk to the system of grinding ABS and other issuances to a halt is far too much for the SEC to bear.

Whilst the US was battling with how to hold the credit rating agencies accountable, the European Union was battling something far more severe. The 'global' nature of the GFC in 2007/09 has always been a contestable notion because, initially, it was a profoundly American and British crisis. Global financial activity certainly reduced, but the impact of the crisis was not truly global. In the European Union, mainly Ireland and then on an associated basis the UK were the hardest hit initially, mostly because of their reliance on the financial sector. Whilst some banks had failed initially and the EU was very much in a recession, 'Europe was still proudly standing'. The European Central Bank had intervened early, leading member states had been able to engineer stimulus packages, 'the euro area had no external deficit, and its aggregate budgetary situation was, if anything, better than that of the United States'. However, in 2009 the executive director for Scandinavia at the IMF had warned in private that the financial crisis would very much become a distinctly European crisis before long, and that proved to be exactly the case.[59] As Ferry describes:

> By 2012 the euro area had fallen into recession even before regaining the level of output it attained in 2007. It was cut in half between a still-prosperous North and a crisis-ridden South, where GDP declined year after year, the rise of unemployment seemed unstoppable, and sovereigns were either cut off from market access or at risk of being rendered insolvent by the very price they were paying to borrow. Private capital had stopped flowing from North to South, forcing the official sector to substitute it. The repair of the banking sector was still a work in progress. The few banks still willing to lend across borders were discouraged from it by the supervisory authorities. Countless summits and ministerial meetings had succeeded in squandering the extraordinary credibility the euro had been credited with. In international gatherings, from IMF to the G20, Europe had been the almost exclusive focus of discussion but was treated with increasing irritation by its international partners. Worst of all, the Europeans had become increasingly wary of each other: those in the North looked down on their partners, letting them know that charity has its limits; those on the South found it increasingly difficult to conceal their anger towards their patronising neighbours.[60]

Europe, as a continent, has a very unique and particular history. Attempting to unify the vast majority of nation states on that continent means attempting to resolve wounds that go back centuries. It also means attempting to unify countries that are dramatically different in many ways, including economically. The capabilities of all the EU members are not equal. In addition to this, the continent of Europe, after playing host to the epicentre of two world wars, brings with it tragic memories of the consequences of failing in those attempts to unify that spread around the globe. Therefore, a crisis in Europe provided the world with a real focus. Within Europe, the disintegration provided the relatively modern political bloc with its first real existential crisis.

The EU therefore sought to steady the ship and progressed down a number of strategic pathways. Massive stimulus packages were developed for member states in greatest need of emergency support, like Greece, whilst others were just about kept above water. The capital markets had been effectively closed to the countries, meaning the EU had to take the leading role. However, the leading politicians within the EU did not see this as a natural occurrence, rather a failure of the signalling system within the capital markets. Within a very short period of time, S&P alone had downgraded *nine* EU members, sparking contagion (S&P were not alone, far from it).[61] Immediately, German Chancellor Angela Merkel said that 'regarding the issue of rating agencies, I think it is important that we do not allow others to take away our own ability to make judgements', whilst the Green Party in the European Parliament declared 'no one can explain why several EU countries have worse credit ratings than the highly indebted US'.[62]

The fact that the US-based credit rating agencies were seen to be taking different approaches to the rating of US sovereign debt and everywhere else did not sit well in Brussels and, as a result, the legislative focus was fully turned to the issue of constraining the potential of the international credit rating agencies. The bloc started the two-phase approach by putting the framework in place first by establishing ESMA (European Securities and Markets Authority) as the supreme regulator for credit rating activities in the bloc.[63] ESMA had been developed a year earlier via Regulation (EU) No 1095/2010, in an attempt to revolutionise the European financial regulatory framework and move past the former model, headed by the Committee of European Securities Regulators. The Regulation said that whilst competent authorities within member states should have tasks delegated to them, the overall responsibility for overseeing the industry had to lie with ESMA. The new regulator had to oversee the registration of agencies, develop technical standards that agencies had to adopt, had to impose fines where appropriate and conduct the necessary investigations, and also make regular on-site visits and produce an annual report. To bridge the Regulation to what would come next, the Commission made clear that there was a need for more investigations into the role and nature of credit rating agencies operating on the continent, and set a timetable for this to be completed.

Those investigations culminated in the 2013 Regulation, which sought to tie the previous two Regulations, and would be accompanied by a Directive a year later that instructed financial participants to stop relying on credit ratings alone for creditworthiness assessments. The final Regulation was hard-hitting and covered a variety of issues that were revealing themselves in the post-GFC era. The Commission essentially put an end to the capabilities of the rating agencies to inject contagion into the bloc, declaring that all registered agencies had to abide by particular timing constraints when publishing ratings, and had to produce a schedule of rating releases in advance:

> In view of the specificities of sovereign ratings and in order to reduce the risk of volatility, it is appropriate and proportionate to require credit rating agencies to publish those ratings only after close of business of the trading venues established in the Union and at least one hour before their opening. On the same basis, it is also appropriate and proportionate that, at the end of December, credit rating agencies should publish a calendar for the following 12 months setting the dates for the publication of sovereign ratings and, corresponding thereto, the dates for the publication of related rating outlooks where applicable. Such dates should be set on a Friday. Only for unsolicited sovereign ratings should the number of publications in the calendar be limited between two and three. Where this is necessary to comply with their legal obligations, credit rating agencies should be allowed to deviate from their announced calendar, while explaining in detail the reasons for such deviation. However, such deviation should not happen routinely.[64]

Furthermore, the prospect of a public credit rating agency was raised and investigative reports started. Also, the ability for an agency to rate groups of countries at one time was taken away. When adjoined to the rulings on the solicitation status of a rating being made public at all times, as well as the requirement that for any changes to a rating, only solicited or public information could be utilised, the Commission had essentially rewritten the rules for sovereign rating development.

The Commission had a number of aims and, arguably, achieved them. However, there were some that would miss their mark, especially when producing rulings that were not grounded in reality. When this book reaches the stage where we apply the concept of signalling to the rating spaces, you will see that the determination by the Commission to increase competition in the sector by suggesting that where two ratings are required, one should be derived from an agency with less than 10% market share, sounds good in principle, but in reality was a complete non-starter, at least in terms of affecting the market share of the so-called Big Three. The similar request by the Commission to set up a rotation-style mechanism that forced the rotating selection of rating agencies upon the market suffered the same fate.

Yet, the Commission did finally turn its attention to the question of liability. Mentioned 18 times in the Regulation, 'liable/liability' was clearly on the agenda. The Commission started by acknowledging that where an investor 'reasonably relied' on the credit rating and then suffered damage on account of an 'infringement' of the 2009 Regulation, there should be an 'adequate right of redress' for that investor. The Regulation says, importantly, that whilst an issuer or investor may have a contractual relationship with the rating agency and therefore take action for breach of contract, methods need to be available for redress more widely. In declaring the level of exposure a credit rating agency would face under the European framework, the Commission declared:

> It should be possible for credit rating agencies to be held liable if they infringe inten-tionally or with gross negligence any obligations imposed on them by Regulation (EC) No 1060/2009. This standard of fault is appropriate because the activity of credit rating involves a certain degree of assessment of complex economic factors and the application of different methodologies may lead to different rating results, none of which can be considered as incorrect. Also, it is appropriate to expose credit rating agencies to potentially unlimited liability only where they breach Regulation (EC) No 1060/2009 intentionally or with gross negligence.[65]

However, the Commission follows this with:

> The investor or issuer claiming damages for an infringement of Regulation (EC) No 1060/2009 should present accurate and detailed information indicating that the credit rating agency has committed such an infringement of that Regulation. This should be assessed by the competent court, taking into consideration that the inves-tor or issuer may not have access to information that is purely within the sphere of the credit rating agency.[66]

Though the Commission provides the context that an investor may not have access to the information they need to provide 'intentional' or 'gross' negli-gence and that a court should take this into account, if a claimant goes to court without the full gamut of information they need to make their case, they will likely not succeed even if they are heard at all. This facet of placing the burden on the investor to pierce the notoriously closed and hardened veil of the rating space is a foundational issue in the official attempts to apply liability. We shall return to this point momentarily.

Before that, however, a step back reveals a more pressing, perhaps systemic, issue. The credit rating agencies did receive an extraordinary amount of legis-lative attention from the Commission, behind perhaps only the banks, which Lehmann suggests is indicative of the Commission being 'CRA obsessed',[67] although this is potentially explained by the threat the industry was causing to the very fundamentals of the multi-state bloc. Nevertheless, the 'obsessed' approach did not lead to an overly impactful approach, the 2013 Regulation's

critics claim. There is a wide acknowledgement that 'the most important innovation of the new regulation is the introduction of a civil liability regime',[68]
although the fact that the imposition was done through the member states'
national legal frameworks has been decried, as Lehmann states: 'But to know
whether a rating agency is liable, one will have to look to Member State law.
Empty lawmaking has never been done more artfully.'[69] So, whilst confirming that the member states will be the dominant vehicle for applying civil
liability,[70] there are two major problems. The first is that, as Picciau explains,
credit ratings are, unlike audits, not (always) necessary for the public offering
of financial instruments and, as such, not all member states even have rating
agencies referenced in their national laws.[71] Worst still, the reality is:

> Although all of the foregoing difficulties are important, they are superseded by
> another, even more fundamental problem. According to Article 2(1) of the CRA
> Regulation, the whole regulation only applies to credit ratings issued by agencies
> registered in the EU. It has, therefore, been concluded in the literature that only
> agencies registered in the EU are subject to civil liability under the Regulation.
> This means that the 'big three' rating agencies would effectively not fall under the
> regulation. All of them have their headquarters in the USA. Although Fitch Ratings
> has a second headquarters in the UK, it is not itself registered in the EU. Rather,
> this function is fulfilled by its subsidiaries in different Member States. The big three
> could thus never be sued under Article 35a CRA Regulation by a European or any
> other investor. It is true that there may be victims with a claim against their sub-
> sidiaries that are established in Europe and registered there. But these subsidiaries
> are not much more than mere letterbox companies. Their main task is to endorse
> ratings issued by their US parent, i.e. to confirm compliance with EU law. The
> CRA Regulation does not require them to dispose of a particular amount of capital
> or of a guarantee by the parent company. In case of a massive damages claim, their
> financial resources will quickly be depleted. If the liability provision in the CRA
> regulation will only hit them and not their parent companies in USA, it would be
> nothing more than a paper tiger.[72]

Whilst clearly critical of the efforts of the Commission, Lehmann here identifies perhaps the fundamental constraint on the legislative potential of the
European Union when dealing with the credit rating agencies who emanate
from the United States: the agencies are foreign entities. They will never be
European at their core and, with that understood, how one can regulate them
needs to be redefined and contextualised differently.

Nevertheless, there are bigger issues at play in the reality of the world.
Those issues all revolve around the same dynamic, namely turning vision into
reality. Nastergard explains for us that, initially, the Commission wanted to
harmonise the approach to applying liability and impose a strict definition of
liability across the continent. However, it would be the British who strongly
opposed such plans, with the Financial Secretary to the Treasury remarking that 'the UK already has rules in place on the liability of credit rating

agencies; they are sufficiently nuanced to be able to hold CRAs liable where appropriate'.[73] The Commission relented and moved away from the approach of applying strict liability as a result, even though in reality the British had a particularly substantial legal framework for such instances of applying civil liability in the financial sector already in place, combined with extensive case law, which other European countries did not necessarily have, as well as being the European host for the American CRAs in London (so, had an interest to protect in the battle of the financial centres); and, to add insult to injury, the British would vote to leave the Union just two years later, leaving the Europeans with, in the field of credit rating regulation at least, the sense of a missed opportunity.

An associated issue is that, in the initial plans of the Commission, there was no mention of an investor having to prove they reasonably relied on a rating in order to bring a claim against the rating.[74] The sentiment here is that market pressure resulted in another retreat by the Commission, and the almost universal understanding of this is that the retreat generated an exceptionally high barrier for claimants against the rating agencies. Mollers and Niedorf say that 'the regulation on the burden of proof is the drawback of the whole liability regime', whilst Picciau simply says that 'there are still significant barriers for investors to overcome' now that the Regulation says that the investor must 'prove the causal connection between the infringement and the injury [and] has to establish reliance and the impact of the alleged violation of the credit rating agency'.[75] There is a problem with this ruling, though: earlier in the Regulation, it declares that entities must no longer rely only on credit ratings, and the Directive that came a year later filters this ruling throughout the European financial system. As Mollers and Niedorf then point out, 'since art.5 requires them (investors) to make their own assessments, it is virtually impossible for them to claim that they still relied on the (outside) rating to an extent that justifies a damage claim'. Explaining further, if an investor's forecast on an entity's creditworthiness is the same as that of a credit rating agency, then the investor does not rely extensively on the credit rating. If the investor's forecast on creditworthiness is *different* from that of a credit rating agency, 'no investor who trusts his own assessment will instead rely on that of the agency as such reliance would imply that he did not sufficiently fulfil his duties laid out in art.4' as well as the myriad fiduciary duties applied to investment managers.[76]

Once we add to this the understanding that an investor, from the outside looking in, has no way of obtaining evidence from a rating agency that would implicate them, the bind that investors find themselves in should they want to claim for damages is ostensibly clear. With the disclosures that a rating agency must make in mind, either in private to a regulator (which only gets publicly published in a codified form) or in public, the options for a claimant are slim. Add to this the issue that all of the Big Three operate via subsidiaries in Europe, then the chances of adequately redressing harm caused by ratings lessens further still. Yet, in the US, the environment was different.

6.   SEEKING A PATHWAY THROUGH TO ACTION

We know already that the Dodd-Frank Act had allowed for liability to be imposed upon the credit rating industry, but that the practical application of that liability had been found wanting. With key market dynamics essentially preventing Congress's will from being applied, attention turned to assisting injured parties to find some sort of redress for the harm caused by rating agencies in the lead-up to the GFC. However, the legal framework set up by the Dodd-Frank Act was not as facilitative as future events would have suggested.

In the Dodd-Frank Act itself, we heard earlier how the Act confirms that claimants must demonstrate that the agencies 'knowingly or recklessly failed' to (i) conduct a reasonable investigation of the rated security against its own stated methodologies or (ii) failed to obtain reasonable verification of the elements of the security in addition to proclamations from the issuing party. This, unsurprisingly, was essentially translated into the European arena by the Commission three years later, but, as was stated above, the American context is very different. One easily understandable fact is that the 'Big Three' are all headquartered in New York City, meaning hiding behind the constraining limits of a subsidiary is not possible in the American context. Another difference is that whilst the whole world seemingly became involved in the deterioration of standards in relation to the securitisation of mortgages, it was predominantly *American-headquartered* entities involved and they were investing in *American mortgages*. These facts bring with them political and legal pressure that is very different from what was being experienced across the Atlantic Ocean.

In 2009, immediately after the peak of the GFC, a legal case was initiated that would eventually change what was thought possible in relation to holding credit rating agencies accountable. It is worth providing some backstory here because, whilst the result was record-breaking, in a sense, the details of the story are so particular and so unique that they are unlikely to become a precedent that we will see replicated again; the consequence of that is that people championing the results of this litigation as a victory for applying liability to the credit rating agencies crucially misunderstand the underlying message that emanates from the story: something so unique means, in reality, liability is not now systemically applied.

The largest public pension fund in the United States, the California Public Employees' Retirement System, also known as CalPERS, had, starting in 2006, invested approximately $1.3 billion into medium-term notes (MTNs) and commercial paper (CP) issued by three specific 'structured investment vehicles' (SIVs):[77] Cheyne Finance, Stanfield Victoria Funding LLC, and Sigma Finance. In extraordinarily simple terms, because the financial architecture in relation to structured finance can get (consciously) complicated, an SIV exists simply to profit from the spread between short-term debt and long-term investment by issuing paper of varying maturities. A product of Citigroup in the late 1980s, the vehicles contain a pool of assets such as asset-backed securities (ABS) or, in the pre-GFC era, residential mortgage-backed securities (RMBS), which are purchased by the bank or asset manager originator by issuing asset-backed commercial paper. Key for our story is that the role of the credit rating agency is absolutely critical to the success of the SIV, for a variety of reasons.

The story of the case reveals key elements to the pathway to liability for credit rating agencies. We have reviewed most of the elements so far in the chapter and, as we draw to a close, the facts of the story will clearly illustrate just how high the bar is for applying liability. The initial complaint from CalPERS starts by detailing the fact that:

> SIVs were corporations with one business activity: issuing debt. Other than the Rating Agencies' evaluation and subsequent credit rating of a SIV, an investor had no access to any information on which to base a judgment of a SIV's creditworthiness. At the time of CalPERS' purchases, the senior debt issued by Cheyne, Stanfield Victoria and Sigma were rated AAA/A-1+ by S&P, and Aaa/P-1 by Moody's. Fitch rated Sigma AAA.[78]

The Dodd-Frank Act enacted the ruling that credit rating agencies must add signifiers to their ratings if they are ratings for structured finance (usually denoted by monikers like 'sf') so that investors knew that the rating for structured finance deals was not based on the historical methodological accuracy that, say, corporate bond ratings were. However, in 2006, this was not the case, and CalPERS, with literally no other way of assessing the underlying quality of what the SIVs were holding and selling, only had ratings to go on that were the same as the most trusted and stable of corporate entities, or as highly rated as US debt. Hopefully, you are making the connection between this story and what happened with Penn Central.

The claim indicated that 'the rating agencies purported to base their ratings of SIVs on (a) the supposedly high quality of the assets contained in the SIV; and (b) the structural mechanisms of SIVs, which were supposed to ensure that a SIV would sell off its underlying assets in order to keep a minimum threshold of capital, and thus keep noteholders' investments safe'. However, credit rating agencies could not have built up a bank of experience in understanding SIVs properly because only 'approximately 28 SIVs have ever been created. The oldest dates back twenty years to 1989. SIVs experienced a growth spike beginning in 2005, when eighteen SIVs were created in the 2005–2007 time period.' Interestingly, the claim referenced the views of a former S&P consultant, who said that 'SIVs came to be nothing more than a mechanism by which investment banks could move exposure to risky assets off their balance sheets. In the consultant's view, SIVs were the "end of the road" for these assets.' Yet, the investors could not know this. What the agencies knew, however, was completely different and absolutely material.

There are two elements to what the rating agencies 'knew' which makes the journey towards applying liability that much clearer. The first element is that the rating agencies 'became actively involved in the creation and ongoing operation of structured finance products like SIVs. Indeed, not only did they help structure the Cheyne, Stanfield Victoria and Signa SIVs here in question, but they were also actively involved in the creation of the structured finance assets held by SIVs, like RMBS and CDOs.' The rating agencies were actively incentivised to rate the products *they had helped design* along with the underlying assets, because they would earn remarkable fees for the rating of an SIV, as well as the associated fees for designing the models (which investors did not know about). Perhaps the real pinch point is that the fees were wholly contingent on the SIV ultimately being offered to investors, further still injecting incentive for rating inflation. The whole process was big business, exemplified by the fact that by 2005, the fees coming from rating (and designing) structured finance deals equated to 41% of Moody's *entire* revenues and, by Q1 of 2007, more than *53%*. As the complaint poignantly remarks: 'for five years in a row (leading to 2007), Moody's had the highest profit margin of any company in the S&P 500.' Not to be outdone as the market-share leader, S&P's revenues from structured finance grew *800%* from 2002 to 2006, with almost half of its 2006 to 2008 growth coming from structured finance rating (and designing) fees. Critically for our story, Fitch was a comparably lesser player, albeit still active and still recording record revenues for the third member of the oligopoly.

The second critical element regarding what the agencies 'knew' was that:

> Cheyne, Stanfield Victoria and Sigma were not available for purchase by the general investor community, but could only be sold to a specific class of investors. The three SIVs were offered only via a private placement as unregistered securities, exempt from registration (and concomitant disclosure requirements) under SEC Rule 144A. By law, Cheyne, Stanfield Victoria and Sigma could be sold only to those who were both 'Qualified Institutional Buyers' (QIBs) under Rule 144A and 'Qualified Purchasers' (QPs) pursuant to the 1940 Investment Act. Public pension funds like CalPERS are one of the few types of investors who qualify as QIBs and QPs.[79]

The claim also went on to show that the rating agencies were actively failing to monitor, investigate, and update their surveillance of the ratings once provided, leaving aside the fact that they were hugely conflicted in designing and providing the rating. All in all, the claim therefore positions several of the key checks in the necessary checklist for applying liability:

- Privity between the claimant and the defendant: the rating agencies knew who would be consuming the ratings as it was a very exclusive list of those legally able to invest.
- The rating agencies had *knowingly or recklessly* failed to conduct a reasonable investigation of the rated security with respect to the factual elements relied upon by its own methodology for evaluating credit risk.
- The rating agencies had *knowingly or recklessly* failed to obtain reasonable verification of such factual elements (which verification may be based on a sampling technique that does not amount to an audit) from other sources that the credit rating agency considered to be competent and that were independent of the issuer and underwriter.
- The rating agencies had *knowingly* conspired to design the products with the issuers of the debt, and knew that the investors had no way of knowing this prior to investing.
- The rating agencies were actively unsure of the quality of the underlying financial products in the SIV, which they also rated and failed to monitor.

Everything for the claimant was in alignment, bar one thing: proof. The Dodd-Frank Act, just like the European Commission's Regulation, coincidentally, made clear that the burden of proof was on the claimant, and that the state of mind could not be inferred and that proof was required. What happened next was something never witnessed before in the credit rating oligopoly.

The complaint that we have just focused on was from CalPERS against all three of the leading agencies. In the *very same year* that the complaint was lodged, 'Fitch settled with CalPERS in 2011. No money changed hands, but Fitch handed over some confidential documents to enable CalPERS to pursue its claims against Moody's and S&P.'[80] Now, critically, CalPERS had completed the liability puzzle. It could prove, via piercing the rating oligopoly, the state of mind of the leading rating agencies. As such, CalPERS demanded a jury trial. Coincidentally, and it will become pertinent in a moment, that same year, in 2011, S&P downgraded the US sovereign rating, a move hitherto unheard of, with S&P being the only rating agency to take such an action. Two years later, in continuing our journey, the CalPERS case, as well as other smaller cases, was picked up by the Department of Justice (DoJ) and, on 5 February 2013, the DoJ sued S&P for fraud in relation to their performance and role in the GFC. The charge, remarkable in itself, alleged that S&P 'engaged in a scheme to defraud investors', and that S&P 'falsely represented that its ratings were objective, independent, and uninfluenced by S&P's relationships with investment banks when, in actuality, S&P's desire for increased revenue and market share led it to favour the interests of these banks over investors'. Then Attorney General Eric Holder simply remarked that 'this alleged conduct is egregious – and it goes to the very heart of the recent financial crisis'.[81] For the lawsuit, the DoJ was looking to recover more than $5 billion in damages for those it was representing.

Probably in one of their most unwise moves, S&P argued that the lawsuit was a direct reaction from the US Government to its downgrading of the sovereign in 2011. Nevertheless, the case would never even come close to a courtroom, as S&P settled with the DoJ, state attorneys, and CalPERS for a grand total of $1.375 billion, the largest monetary settlement on record in the credit rating arena. Furthermore, Attorney General Holder was adamant that S&P would officially retract their allegation of the US seeking vengeance for their downgrade, saying ultimately that the allegation from S&P was 'utter nonsense' and that having S&P formally retract was 'important to me'. CalPERS had achieved half of its objective and summarily went after Moody's, which the DoJ would eventually take over too. On exactly the same basis, Moody's would also settle for a grand total of $864 million. All in all, CalPERS would suggest that they managed to resolve the harm caused to it by the rating agencies, after seven years of litigation.

And there you have it, as they say. Liability was ultimately imposed, and the resultant penalty, albeit by settlement, was a record one. However, the 'tale of the tape' does not reveal the reality of the situation. If it were not for Fitch essentially acting in their own best interest against the interest of the oligopoly, liability *could not* have been applied. This reveals two conclusions. The first is that it suggests that the oligopoly is really a duopoly because, theoretically, Fitch should have put the oligopoly ahead of its own interests. Second is the realisation that the whole push for liability in the rating sector, across the whole globe, came down to one instance of splitting allegiances in the credit rating oligopoly, in *one* jurisdiction; in other jurisdictions, there have been no penalties of any sort for the performance of the rating agencies in the lead-up to the GFC. Let me add to this, as one final thought, that if you think the record penalty affected the leading two credit rating agencies, then you are massively mistaken. I demonstrated in my PhD thesis quite clearly that the allowance and growth of credit rating agencies providing ancillary services during this boon in securitisation fees (lest we forget, fees that were also for *designing* the SIVs in secret, as well as advising on the underlying structured finance products) *entirely offset* the pain of the record settlements: the profits garnered from the provision of ancillary services alone dwarfs the collective $2.2 billion the Big Two paid.[82]

Ultimately, applying liability in the credit rating space is a double-edged sword: it is possible, but so specific and unlikely that it is almost illusory. The question we must ask ourselves in this book is whether that reality is translatable across rating industries and sectors, or specific to credit rating.

7.   CONCLUSION

This chapter had a simple aim of seeking to prepare the ground for our analysis of the ESG rating space to come later in the book. The nascency of the ESG rating space, and the regulation of it, does not exist in a vacuum. Even without the fact that all of the Big Three rating agencies, and others, have started offering products and services within the ESG rating space, the similarities between the two industries are clearly evident. From similar practices and methodological developments to translatable ambitions for the future of the ESG rating space built upon the credit rating model, the historic credit rating space can and does provide plenty of insight into the underlying dynamics that have and will continue to affect the ESG rating space. For that reason, we started this book by focusing on the credit rating industry from within the perspective of applying liability in the space.

A quasi-historical analysis quickly revealed that the early credit reporting agencies, the forefathers of the credit rating industry, had synergistically grown alongside the concept of liability and its application. The issue of liability was front and centre for the early mercantile agencies, for reasons that apply today when one takes a step back. The early agencies had two main junctures of concern, namely that their products were invasive and that they were also subjective in nature. The marketplace was not overly welcoming of the private endeavour to resolve the fundamental asymmetric problem that resulted from the expansion of the Americas. Media reaction, private reaction, and also judicial reaction was almost unanimous in its condemnation of the approaches taken by the early mercantile agencies, who deployed rather callous strategies to avoid being held liable for their products and their performance. Nevertheless, in what upon reflection is a constant theme for the industries, the *need* always outranked anything else. Meeting a systemic requirement in such a simple manner is the protection that the agencies have always needed, irrespective of what form the industry takes at a given time. Early scandals were brushed aside, and in adapting to the times, the industry grew almost synergistically with the American, and later the global, economy.

The recognition of their offering of a systemically vital product, first from the judiciary and then from the formalised state via regulation, had consequences. Later in the book we shall apply the theory of signalling to the worlds of ESG and credit ratings more directly, but even here the idea of sending and receiving signals is appropriate. What message did the actions of the Comptroller in the 1930s send the early credit rating agencies? What message did the eventual protection from an adversarial judiciary send to the industries?

The message was that there was an understanding that the systemic requirement would always be taken into account. Now, how that message is received and interpreted is another question entirely, because it could be interpreted in a variety of ways. It could be seen as an endorsement of the service, but that the acknowledgement of faults and issues meant that overstepping one's boundary was certainly of concern. Or, it could be received that the systemic importance means there are no boundaries. If heinous strategies to defend against liability are all fine, why not seek to monetise that systemic position?

In the 1960s, we saw the first attempt at systemic monetisation from an associated industry. The National Credit Office's behaviour, approach, culture, and performance all signal that economic rent-taking was in full effect. The NCO knew they were the only service in town, that investors were being systemically funnelled into their system, and that the most profitable route would be to side with the issuers of the debt against the position of the investors. They knew all this and did it anyway, quite simply because they could. In spite of any seeming reputational concern, the NCO was deemed to be dispensable to the larger parent of Dun & Bradstreet, who knew that Moody's was (a) more reputable in the eyes of the public, (b) more established, and (c) ready to step into any void the distinct emptying of standards at the NCO would have caused. Low and behold, within just five years, the credit rating agencies had been installed, via regulation, into the system of finance just as technology took hold and fundamentally expanded the capital markets as a structure. What message had all this sent to the rating agencies?

Irrespective of the message, what was received was essentially 'the rules of the game'. Not providing a resolution to an asymmetrical problem was simply not an option. However, in the era of the GFC, the moral hazard was more pronounced: there was no Moody's or S&P waiting in the wings to take advantage from the deterioration of standards or reputation. There was simply no alternative, and one can strongly argue that the rating agencies knew this. They had successfully interpreted 'the rules to the game' to their own advantage. Their behaviour in the lead-up to the crisis can lead to no other conclusion than this.

The scale of the agencies' collusion with big business against society forced the hands of the state. To not act after such a monumental extraction of wealth from the public, in an operation entirely at odds with the publicised tenets of capitalism (which, in reality, are simply not evident, as the public will always be the lender of last resort), would have left the state vulnerable and its authority in question. That environment cannot be divorced from the story because it is indicative of the results that were reached. Rather than applying liability in a systemic and meaningful way, the decision to apply liability was done in a reactive manner from within a GFC stance. The results were predictable. Not only did the main attempt by the US Congress fail the moment it went live – so much so that the main securities regulator had to actively disregard the congressional order and has yet to reverse course 13 years later – but the 'success' of the DoJ's settlement is, upon inspection, a failure. That success is a failure because of three aspects. First, it is based on circumstances so unique that it will never be repeated. Second, it sets the bar so high that anything other than outright fraud and a breakdown in oligopolistic unity will fail to clear the bar. Third, it sent a resounding message to the rating agencies for their respective futures: your failure will not result in your fatality. The collective $2 billion in settlement fee is nowhere close to what the agencies made since the turn of the century, and have continued to make after the GFC.

Therefore, there are a variety of conclusions. In the credit rating space, liability has not been applied. Furthermore, attempts to apply liability have routinely failed. On top of this, applying liability outside of the US, even in a developed region like Europe, is essentially a non-starter. Those understandings, when paired to the understanding of the centrality and systemic importance of the concept of credit ratings, provides for a really stark consideration. The picture is one of essential lawlessness with a veneer of order for the very first time in a long time. The impact of this is considerable. For the rating agencies, the message of being able to continue unimpeded has been received. For regulators, the constraints have been made abundantly clear. For legislators, the reality of the rating space has been illustrated clearly, but whether they pay attention is another matter entirely. There has not been another systemic need for the regulatory or legislative consideration of the rating agencies since the GFC, but there is a comparable case study: ESG ratings. We shall see in this book that lessons are not being learned from the credit rating experience, indicating a deep flaw within the relationship between public sector and private sector when it comes to ratings and resolving the informational asymmetry that affects every aspect of the relationship between business and society. Yet, before we do that, we need to understand some of the underlying dynamics that will affect the regulation of the ESG rating space, and to do that we must understand the liability question from within the parameters of understanding ESG as a concept.

NOTES

1. Alan R White, *Grounds of Liability: An Introduction to the Philosophy of Law* (Clarendon Press 1985).
2. Daniel Cash, *A Modern Credit Rating Agency: The Story of Moody's* (Routledge 2024).
3. Daniel Cash, *Sustainability Rating Agencies vs. Credit Rating Agencies: The Battle to Serve the Mainstream Investor* (Palgrave Macmillan 2021).
4. Rowena Olegario, *A Culture of Credit: Embedding Trust and Transparency in American Business* (Harvard University Press 2009) 77.

5.   R.W. Hidy, 'Credit Rating before Dun and Bradstreet' (1939) 13 Bulletin of the Business Historical Society 6 81.
6.   Olegario (n 4).
7.   Martin Ruef, *Between Slavery and Capitalism: The Legacy of Emancipation in the American South* (Princeton University Press 2014) 140.
8.   Cash (n 2) 28.
9.   Bertram Wyatt-Brown 'God and Dun & Bradstreet, 1841–1851' (1966) 40 The Business History Review 4 432–50, 445.
10.   Olegario (n 4) 72.
11.   James H Madison, 'The Evolution of Commercial Credit Reporting Agencies in Nineteenth-Century America' (1974) 48 The Business History Review 2 164–86, 178.
12.   Marc Flandreau and Gabriel G. Mesevage, 'The Untold History of Transparency: Mercantile Agencies, the Law, and the Lawyers (1851–1916)' (2014) 15 Enterprise & Society 2 213–51, 214.
13.   ibid 216.
14.   ibid.
15.   Madison (n 11) 169.
16.   Scott A Sandage, *Born Losers: A History of Failure in America: A History of Failure in America* (Harvard University Press 2006) 183.
17.   Madison (n 11) 181.
18.   Frank Partnoy, 'The Siskel and Ebert of Financial Markets?: Two Thumbs Down for the Credit Rating Agencies' (1999) 77 Washington University Law Quarterly 3 619, 681.
19.   Jonathan R. Macey, 'The Demise of the Reputational Model in Capital Markets: The Problem of the "Last Period Parasites"' (2010) 60 Syracuse Law Review 428.
20.   Frank Partnoy, 'The Paradox of Credit Ratings' in Richard M Levich, Giovanni Majnoni, and Carmen Reinhart (eds), *Ratings, Rating Agencies and the Global Financial System* (Kluwer Academic Press 2002) 70.
21.   Daniel Cash, 'Credit Rating Agency Regulation Since the Financial Crisis: The Evolution of the 'Regulatory Licence' Concept' in Daniel Cash and Robert Goddard, *Regulation and the Global Financial Crisis: Impact, Regulatory Responses, and Beyond* (Routledge 2021) 162.
22.   Charles Adams, Donald J. Mathieson, and Garry Schinasi, *International Capital Markets: Developments, Prospects, and Key Policy Issues* (International Monetary Fund 1999) 200.
23.   Bianca Mostacatto, 'Eliminating Regulatory Reliance on Credit Ratings: Restoring the Strength of Reputational Concerns' (2013) 24 Stanford Law and Policy Review 99, 119.
24.   ibid.
25.   See: Marc Flandreau, Norbert Gaillard, and Frank Packer, 'To err is human: US rating agencies and the interwar foreign government debt crisis' (2011) 15 European Review of Economic History 495–538; Marc Flandreau and Joanna K Sławatyniec, 'Understanding rating addiction: US courts and the origins of rating agencies' regulatory licence (1900–1940)' (2013) 20 Financial History Review 3 237–57; Marc Flandreau and Gabriel G Mesevage, 'The separation of information and lending and the rise of the rating agencies in the USA (1841–1907)' (2014) 62 Scandinavian Economic History Review 3 213–242; Marc Flandreau and Gabriel G Mesevage, 'The Untold History of Transparency: Mercantile

Agencies, the Law, and the Lawyers (1851–1916)' (2014) 15 Enterprise and Society 2 213–51.

26. Flandreau and Mesevage (Separation) (n 25) 214.
27. Scott Sandage, *Born Losers: A History of Failure in America* (Harvard University Press 2005).
28. Flandreau and Sławatyniec (n 25) 239.
29. Avner Shaked and John Sutton, 'Natural Oligopolies' (1983) 51 Econometrica 5.
30. Ulrich G Schroeter, 'Credit Ratings and Credit Rating Agencies' in Gerard Caprio (Ed), *Handbook of Key Global Financial Markets, Institutions, and Infrastructure* (Elsevier 2013).
31. ibid 387.
32. ibid.
33. Gianluca Mattarocci, *The Independence of Credit Rating Agencies: How Business Models and Regulators Interact* (Academic Press 2013).
34. Cash (n 2) see final chapter.
35. Partnoy (n 18) 648.
36. Robert Hudson, Alan Colley, Mark Largan, *The Capital Markets and Financial Management in Banking* (Routledge 2013) 175.
37. U.S. Senate, *The Financial Collapse of the Penn Central Company: Staff Report of the SEC to the Special Subcommittee on Investigations* (GPO 1972) 287.
38. ibid.
39. Robin E Phelan, 'Recent Developments in Corporation, Partnership and Securities Law' (1976) 13 Bulletin of the Section on Corporation, Banking and Business Law: State Bar of Texas 2, 6.
40. Cash (n 2) see Chapter III.
41. Eva H Wirten, *No Trespassing: Authorship, Intellectual Property Rights, and the Boundaries of Globalisation* (The University of Toronto Press 2004) 61.
42. John (Xuefeng) Jiang, Mary H Stanford, and Yuan Xie, 'Does it matter who pays for bond ratings? Historical Evidence' [2012] 105 Journal of Financial Economics 607, 620.
43. Mathias Lehmann, 'Civil Liability of Rating Agencies – an Insipid Sprout from Brussels' (2016) 11 Capital Markets Law Journal 1 60–83, 62.
44. US Senate, *Wall Street and the Financial Crisis: Anatomy of a Financial Collapse* (GPO 2011).
45. As just one mildly representative example, see: Daniel Cash and Robert Goddard, *Regulation and the Global Financial Crisis: Impact, Regulatory Responses, and Beyond* (Routledge 2021).
46. For this argument, see the intervention of Senator Wallison in National Commission on the Causes of the Financial and Economic Crisis in the United States, *The Financial Crisis Inquiry Report* (GPO 2011).
47. *Credit Rating Agency Reform Act of 2006* 120 Stat. 1327.
48. Regulation (EC) No 1060/2009.
49. Lehmann (n 43) 78.
50. Mohammed Hemraj, *Credit Rating Agencies: Self-Regulation, Statutory Regulation and Case Law Regulation in the United States and European Union* (Springer 2015) 139.
51. Chiara Picciau, 'The evolution of the liability of credit rating agencies in the United States and in the European Union: Regulation after the Crisis' (2018) 2 ECFR 339–402, 356.

52. Frank Partnoy, *Rethinking Regulation of Credit Rating Agencies: An Institutional Perspective* (Council of Institutional Investors 2009) 12.
53. Picciau (n 51) 359.
54. ibid 361.
55. Norbert Gaillard and Michael Waibel, 'The Icarus Syndrome: How Credit Rating Agencies Lost Their Quasi Immunity' (2018) 71 SMU Law Review 4 1077–1116.
56. Nan S Ellis and Steven B Dow, 'Attaching Criminal Liability to Credit Rating Agencies: Use of the Corporate Ethos Theory of Criminal Liability' (2014) 17 University of Pennsylvania Journal of Business Law 167, 209.
57. SEC, *Response of the Office of Chief Counsel Division of Corporation Finance* (2010) https:// www .sec .gov/ divisions/ corpfin/ cf -noaction/ 2010/ ford072210 -1120.htm.
58. Americans for Financial Reform, *Letters to Regulators: Letter Calling on the SEC to Rescind the 2010 Ford Motor Credit No-Action Letter* (2022) https:// ourfinancialsecurity .org/2022/01/letters-to-regulators-letter-calling-on-the-sec -to-rescind-the-2010-ford-motor-credit-no-action-letter/.
59. Jean Pisani-Ferry, *The Euro Crisis and its Aftermath* (Oxford University Press 2011) ix.
60. ibid x.
61. Marilyn Geewax and Eyder Peralta, 'S&P downgrades the credit of nine European countries, including France' (2012) NPR (Jan 13) https:// www .npr .org/sections/thetwo-way/2012/01/13/145178453/s-p-downgrades-france-deals -a-blow-to-eurozone.
62. David Bocking, 'Europe seeks to free itself from Rating Agencies' grip' (2011) Spiegel (July 6) https:// www .spiegel .de/ international/ business/ fear -of -junk -status-europe-seeks-to-free-itself-from-rating-agencies-grip-a-772733.html.
63. Regulation (EU) No 513/2011.
64. Regulation (EU) No 462/2013 (42).
65. ibid (33).
66. ibid (34).
67. Lehmann (n 43) 61.
68. Thomas M.J. Mollers and Charis Niedorf, 'Regulation and Liability of Credit Rating Agencies – A More Efficient European Law?' (2014) 11 ECFR 333, 346.
69. Lehmann (n 43) 68.
70. Aline Darbellay, *Regulating Credit Rating Agencies* (Edward Elgar 2013) 80.
71. Chiara Picciau, 'The civil liability of credit rating agencies to investors in the EU' in Olha O Cherednychenko and Mads Andenas, *Financial Regulation and Civil Liability in European Law* (Edward Elgar 2020) 184.
72. Lehmann (n 43) 81.
73. Emil Nastergard, 'Does Member State Law Make Article 35a of the EU Regulation on Credit Rating Agencies Redundant?' (2015) University of Oslo Faculty of Law Legal Studies Research Paper Series No. 2015-04, 2.
74. Mollers and Niedorf (n 68) 347.
75. Picciau (n 51) 386.
76. Mollers and Niedorf (n 68) 347.
77. For a whole-life examination of the securitisation process as it was developed for the GFC, see: Markus Krebsz, *Securitisation and Structured Finance Post Credit Crunch: A Best Practice Deal Lifecycle Guide* (John Wiley & Sons 2011).

78. Complaint for Negligent Misrepresentation Under Common Law & California Civil Code §§ 1709 & 1710 & Negligent Interference with Prospective Economic Advantage at 23, Cal. Pub. Employees' Ret. Sys. v. Moody's Corp., No. CGC-09-490241, 19.

79. ibid 82.

80. Dale Kasler 'CalPERS cleared to sue ratings agencies' (2014) Sacramento Bee (Sept. 15) http://www.sacbee.com/news/business/article2609814.html.

81. Department of Justice, 'Department of Justice Sues Standard & Poor's for Fraud in Rating Mortgage-Backed Securities in the Years Leading up to the Financial Crisis' (2013) https://www.justice.gov/opa/pr/department-justice-sues-standard -poor-s-fraud-rating-mortgage-backed-securities-years-leading.

82. Daniel Cash, *The Regulation of Credit Rating Agencies: An Analysis of the Transgressions of the Rating Industry and a Measured Proposal for Reform* (2016) Durham e-Theses – http://etheses.dur.ac.uk/11838/.

3. The relationship between ESG and the law

1. INTRODUCTION

This chapter starts with several caveats. The interrelationship between 'ESG' and 'the law' is not a homogenous one. It is growing organically in different regions according to different legal and structural cultures, perhaps as it should. The underlying essence of what 'ESG' is, or at least is supposed to be, is debatable. Some may see ESG as an evolution of CSR (corporate social responsibility), whereby corporate entities not only seek to make profit, but also do good at the same time. Others may see ESG purely as a baseline consideration of corporate entities that they almost naturally factor into the considerations, alongside financial concerns. In that understanding, an investment manager may, for example, seek to understand the investee company's relationship with its communities, as well as its financial performance. These 'extreme' ends of the spectrum are perhaps not ends of a spectrum at all, but for us they provide us with a simplistic understanding of the multiplicity of understanding, which quickly becomes problematic when developed within a rigid structure like the law.

While this chapter will not aim to unpick the nuances of what ESG was, or is supposed to be, there are some questions that can be asked which will be helpful. What ESG was supposed to be originally can be best answered by the author of the foreword of this book, but others tend to attempt definitions in relation to other concepts, like investing. For example, Matos suggests that the separate elements (the 'E', the 'S', and the 'G') all relate to the company's impact on something 'external' to itself, like the natural ecosystem, its workforce, or its (internal) strategy for organising its constituents.[1] This is probably the most obvious definition and relates directly to the concept of 'impact', however one would like to imagine that concept. However, MSCI (who we will meet more formally in the next chapter) acknowledge that the term ESG is often conflated with 'sustainable investing', but ultimately declare that, for them, ESG is irrevocably linked to investing.[2] This becomes problematic when we learn about MSCI's approach to ESG ratings, a field within which they are one of the leaders, but I digress ahead of the next chapter. The Principles for

Responsible Investment vehicle within the UN calls this linkage that MSCI describes 'ESG integration', which then becomes one of many investment methods that can be used (alongside such techniques as 'screening', for example, where an investor will purposively remove certain categories of investments from their universe of prospective investments).[3] Ultimately, the linkage between the concepts of ESG and investing are strong,[4] but for this author the focus is more on the underlying sentiment, the driving principles, and the arguably philosophical underpinnings and eventual consequences.

It should not be downplayed that ESG is now considered mainstream, or at least perceived to be, for a reason. It is the latest in a long line of endeavours to make capitalistic business more considerate of the environment within which they operate. To suggest that the mainstreaming of the concept of ESG is directly and irrevocably linked to the Global Financial Crisis (GFC) is not a novel suggestion, with market participants being quite clear that 'the global financial crisis pushed ESG principles to the forefront, which would not have occurred as rapidly without the catalyst of the crisis'.[5] Yet, this understanding is complicated. If the rise of 'ESG' is a response to the GFC, even though it was imagined just beforehand, then there are associated questions to ask, like, 'can ESG be an effective, or even an appropriate, remedy for the damage caused by the GFC?', or 'if ESG is the solution, is it too close to the problem?'

We saw in the last chapter how investors had hurtled towards the RMBS market at a rate of knots. Whether or not they were fed into a mincing machine, as the post-GFC congressional investigations appeared to indicate, is irrelevant in a sense, because a lot of investment is done by people who have specific duties to uphold when they do so. We will cover their duties later on in much more detail, but if ESG as a concept is supposed to be a better way of operating, then the question becomes whether there are more impactful ways of achieving better corporate practice than encouraging corporate entities to consider more than the financial aspects in front of them. Conversely, ESG as a concept may be iterative, or incremental in that it is the first stage of a journey moving corporate mentalities away from the core mentality that allowed the GFC to take place.

Yet, ESG affects multiple elements of the traditional business environment. There is a duality in its effect which interlinks to a duality we shall uncover in the next chapter relating to the utility of ESG ratings. That duality in terms of effect relates to the importance of ESG to a company's external-facing endeavours (disclosure), and a company's internal-related endeavours (duties). Even the concept of duties, as we shall see, is further decompartmentalised, because there is a distinct difference between so-called 'directors' duties' and the relationship between a principal and an agent, especially in the realm of investment, whereby the new modality for modern capitalism is housed within the concept of an 'institutional investor', like a pension fund or a money manager;

those managers have distinct relationships with those they manage money for, and that relationship brings with it particular rules and responsibilities, which differ somewhat from the rules and responsibilities that govern the relationship between a director and the company they are directing.

As one can see from the above, it all has the potential to become very complicated, very quickly. Yet, any complications should be cleared up by the time we are finished with the next chapter, because the growing role of ESG ratings, as I will position to you, provides the necessary context to all of these intertwined issues. What is an important underlying force is the *pressure* being applied to the financial sector. That pressure, to do things *differently*, has a variety of consequences. The one we are concerned with is how that pressure will force parties to *signal* differently, and this book argues that ESG rating agencies are becoming critical signals with which parties can communicate with one another. Yet, that pressure is also creating behaviours which exemplify the difficult nature of adapting a historic culture to the new era of planetary consideration. That pressure will be evident throughout the chapter.

Before we continue, however, there are several caveats that are needed. The first, and perhaps most obvious, is that tackling ESG as a concept is a very particular and nuanced endeavour and, as such, different jurisdictions will naturally take different approaches to it. Because the concept of ESG is fundamentally intertwined with business, the underlying cultural aspects to how one jurisdiction may view best business practices may differ from another jurisdiction. This chapter, and the book, is not designed to generate appropriate multi-jurisdictional analyses on ESG legislation and regulation. That has been done by other, much more competent, scholars, but even those analyses have within core difficulties. For instance, the pace of change in the sector, and in terms of what ESG applies to, means that academic analysis simply cannot keep up, especially when the publication processes are taken into consideration. Also, the incredible breadth of impact and exposure that the concept of ESG has in relation to the business world means producing effective multi-jurisdictional analyses would take volumes, not just one book. However, there are overarching trends which we will use in this chapter to demonstrate more existential aims and markers for ESG progression. By splitting the focus between the main pillars of disclosure and duties, and then focusing mostly on the American and European endeavours in those fields, the book has a slight chance of painting a representative picture, although that aim comes with massive asterisks. It is fully acknowledged that the European/ Anglo-American viewpoint is not the only one that exists, nor are they the only ones capable of impacting global trends. Yet, the rate of development within those jurisdictions on key elements of ESG data generation and analysis are perhaps indicative of developed economies that can afford to consider such elements so early on, relatively speaking. Other jurisdictions, including the major Asian economies, as well as places like Australia and Canada, are seeking to really catch up to the likes of the European Union who are, as we shall see, streets ahead of anywhere else in terms of formalising this forced change in corporate culture. Furthermore, the differing legal underpinnings for our analysis of disclosure and duty-related developments are well represented in the small jurisdictional sample chosen for the chapter, with both common and civil law jurisdictions represented.

2.   KEY LEGAL CONSIDERATIONS: DISCLOSURE

This chapter is focusing on disclosure and duties as concepts for one particular reason. This is because seeing ESG as a form of informational movement helps in understanding the ecosystem that it affects. For example, it is not good enough just for companies to 'do better', or even attempt to do better; they have to instead be able to show *how* they are doing better, or at least attempting to do so. This is simply because of the same asymmetric problem we looked at in relation to the role of credit rating agencies. The systemic role of a company is a central one that feeds into the capabilities of so many other parts of the modern societal ecosystem.

For example, a company must be able to show that they are trying to do better to satisfy those tasked with regulating the corporate spaces and, crucially, do so in a way that is decipherable, comparable, and verifiable. A company must also be able show their current and prospective customers what they are doing, and how they are doing it. Also, a company usually operates on securing outside investment (in a variety of forms) and such investors would usually need such information to decide whether the investment opportunity is worth it or not. For investors, especially the most systemically important investors, the need for a proper information flow is doubled, in the sense that they themselves need the information from companies to make sound and proper investment decisions, but then they themselves must also produce information to allow others to understand their own decision-making processes and approaches.

It is at this point that I hope you, as a reader, can see the connectedness between all of the subjects this book is and will look at. The informational flows, asymmetrical problems that arise, and the solutions for those problems, run through almost every corporate scenario. Especially when one injects the subjectivity inherent within ESG into the equation, everything becomes that bit more complicated, that bit more nuanced, and ultimately that bit more asymmetrical. This is why this book is focusing on the role of ESG rating agencies and doing so from within a signalling theory perspective, in an attempt to articulate and illustrate this underlying dynamic. Yet, before we get to those analyses, let us understand first the development of the concept of ESG and how it is being governed, and also legally driven. To start with, the concept of 'disclosing' information is one that has been applied to various stages and sectors of the informational flow that nourishes the financial sector.

It is worth starting with the EU, purely because of the scale of their efforts in this particular sector in recent years. It is widely acknowledged that their efforts in the EU are unmatched in terms of scale and ambition, with other jurisdictions only now seeking to catch up and apply their own versions of the standards being developed within the European bloc; Moloney indicates that 'the EU's standards relating to sustainability disclosures generally are currently the highest and also the most wide-ranging internationally'.[6] This is likely because the European Commission, for quite some time, has been embarking upon a systemic cultural change and implementing a variety of regulations, directives, and technical standards to that end. The modern initiatives that we will cover very shortly have a solid foundation that spans back more than two decades in the EU, perhaps indicating the early-adopter status that is revealing itself now in internationally mature initiatives that are setting the EU apart from its international peers.

In 1999, the Treaty of Amsterdam entered force, enshrining sustainable development as an overarching objective of the European Union.[7] The Treaty sought to simplify elements relating to all manner of things affecting European development, but in particular for us, sought to simplify decision-making processes around environmental policy as a bloc. It identified that *integration* was a key method of achieving sustainable development across a multicultural bloc of countries, in the sense of integrating environmental protection requirements into the definition and implementation of the Union's overarching policies. The Treaty also:

> strengthened the framework created by the 1986 SEA (Single European Act) for free movement, reflecting the need to take account of issues of vital importance for society such as the environment, public health or consumer protection. The EC Treaty now requires all proposals by the Commission to be based on a high level of environmental protection.[8]

The Treaty of Amsterdam built on numerous 'phases' across the EU's history, with specific reference to the developments of the Single European Act in 1987, and the more nuanced Treaty of Maastricht in 1993 that made headway by specifically referring to the environment in key sectors of its text. Yet, it was the Treaty of Amsterdam that saw significant developments, with the drafters of the Treaty being noted to have been 'particularly sensitive to the idea of sustainable development'.[9]

In a more general sense over and above the concept of environmental protection, Notaro muses that it is not beyond the realm of reason to suggest that the European drafters would have been acutely aware of supranational developments, and therefore began to act accordingly:

> A similar inter-connection and parallelism can be noticed with regard to the development of the notion of sustainable development at the international and European levels. As mentioned *supra*, already in 1987 the Brundtland Report 'Our Common Future' has given a definition of sustainable development as a means to reconcile environmental protection and economic growth and had provided a major input to the development of international environmental law. It is not difficult to image that (at least some of) the drafters of the Single European Act, who introduced in 1987 for the first time in the EC Treaty an environmental legal basis, were knowledgeable about and sensitive to this as well as to other important developments in international environmental law in between the Stockholm and Rio Conferences.
>
> In the same vein, it is not surprising that the Maastricht Treaty, in 1992, referred to the respect of the environment in its objectives and mentioned explicitly the EC environment policy and the idea of sustainability. Moreover, the EC 1993 Fifth Environment Action Programme ('Towards Sustainability'), adopted shortly after the Rio Conference, testifies already in its title to the impact that the 1992 Rio Conference had on EC environment policy.[10]

The EU therefore has a history of seeking to be up to date with developments regarding sustainability, but recently the pendulum has started to turn towards the EU being early-adopters and market-setting leaders with regards to sustainability practices, frameworks, and approaches.

The EU had already initiated the NFRD (Non-Financial Reporting Directive) in 2014, which required large companies to have to publish information related to a variety of issues, ranging from environmental matters and social matters, as well as human rights, through to anti-corruption efforts and board diversity, amongst others.[11] The NFRD applied to entities with more than 500 employees, and captured the likes of listed companies, banks, and insurance companies within its parameters, totalling nearly 12,000 entities in total. Yet, to complement this effort and go much further, the Commission launched its 'Action Plan: Financing Sustainable Growth' (Action Plan) in March 2018.[12] The Action Plan had several distinct aims, amongst which were:

1. Reorient capital flows towards sustainable investment in order to achieve sustainable and inclusive growth;
2. Manage financial risks stemming from climate change, resource depletion, environmental degradation and social issues; and
3. Foster transparency and long-termism in financial and economic activity.[13]

Within the Action Plan were ten distinct objectives, which would be achieved via several legal vehicles. The ten objectives were:

1. Establishing an EU classification system for sustainability activities (which would become the EU Taxonomy for Sustainable Activities);
2. Creating standards and labels for green financial products;
3. Fostering investment in sustainable projects;
4. Incorporating sustainability when providing investment advice;
5. Developing sustainability benchmarks;
6. Better integrating sustainability in ratings and research;
7. Clarifying institutional investors and asset managers' duties;
8. Incorporating sustainability in prudential requirements;
9. Strengthening sustainability disclosure and accounting rule-making; and
10. Fostering sustainable corporate governance and attenuating short-termism in capital markets.

This was to be achieved via a Taxonomy for Sustainable Activities, which aimed to 'establish the conditions and the framework to create, over time, a unified classification system on what can be considered environmentally sustainable economic activities. This [was] widely seen as a first and essential enabling step in the overall effort to channel investment into sustainable activities.'[14] The taxonomy was put into place via regulation in 2020 and confirmed that an economic activity would be considered as environmentally sustainable if it met at least one of the following environmental objectives (while doing no significant harm to any of them):

• Climate change mitigation;
• Climate change adaptation;
• The sustainable use and protection of water and marine resources;
• The transition to a circular economy;
• Pollution prevention and control;
• The protection and restoration of biodiversity and ecosystems.

As stated earlier, this was seen as an important first step in the road to making the whole European economy sustainable in nature. As Busch comments:

> when is a product or business 'green'? That is something we must agree on first. After all, if we in Europe do not have a shared understanding of what is ecologically sustainable, how can we expect to arrange for the supply and demand of green capital to be better matched in Europe?[15]

As Busch continues, 'once we have a shared understanding of what is ecologically sustainable, the next step will be to arrange for financial intermediaries to integrate sustainability considerations into their investment policy and advice, and to provide transparency to the investing public about the extent to which they do this.' It is within the objective of developing a framework to achieve this that the European Commission has developed the SFDR, or the Sustainable Finance Disclosure Regulation.

Essentially, the SFDR:

> obliges financial market participants to disclose informational on material risks a company's activities may pose to the environment and people as well as material risks that environmental factors, including regulatory constraints for environmental and social protection purposes, may have on the company's financial health and prospects – the so-called 'double-materiality' concept.[16]

Yet, it is perhaps easier to understand it by the concept of the SFDR applying to investment firms and advisers. As Busch illustrates so clearly:

> Recital (10) SFDR states that the legislation aims to reduce information asymmetries in principal-agent relationships with regards to (i) the integration of sustainability risks, (ii) the consideration of adverse sustainability impacts and (iii) the promotion of environmental or social characteristics as well as sustainable investment by means of pre-contractual and ongoing disclosures to end investors, acting as principals, by financial market participants or financial advisers, acting as agents on behalf of principals.[17]

The European Commission had identified that the act of investing, and the role of the institutional investor, was now fundamentally intertwined with the concept of modern capitalism. This is despite the EU having a particularly different corporate composition from their peers (the EU hosts a large number of SMEs rather than large corporates, like the United States, for example). Injecting control into how institutional investors took their decisions, by mandating communicative standards that could allow for oversight, became the order of the day in Brussels.

The SFDR is a complex organism, which is not surprising given its regulatory targets. To simplify our understanding, it is easier to simply say that the Regulation pushed for subjects to align their activities to three particular categories, which have been classified under three articles within the Regulation: Article 6, Article 8, and Article 9. The text of Regulation (EU) 2019/2088 can get complicated in places, so there have been myriad attempts to simplify the codification system, with people tending to label Article 8 funds as 'light green', and Article 9 funds as 'dark green'. Very simply, the differing categories are as follows:

- *Article 6 funds:* Funds without a sustainability scope or focus.
- *Article 8 funds:* Funds that promote environmental or social characteristics.
- *Article 9 funds:* Funds that have sustainable investment as their objective.

The differentiation actually lies in the *promotion* and marketing around the funds, not the underlying integration of sustainability into the fund. This is because the integration of sustainability simply applies across all funds, but those that have particular characteristics that are then used to promote that fund to prospective consumers must have evidence to support their claims. The modern focus is really on the intersection between marketing and green claims, often referred to as 'greenwashing', with jurisdictions around the world beginning to turn their attention to the phenomenon. The EU formally included this in their legislative effort with the SFDR, but it sits against a much larger backdrop of challenging greenwashing behaviour in and around the financial sector (though greenwashing spreads much further than the financial sector).

The centrality of institutional investment, and its consequent ability to affect whole societies, is the core of the reason why the EU focused so much upon building and enacting the SFDR. We shall focus on the principal–agent dynamic later in the chapter, but one can see clearly here that it sits right at the heart of everything in the modern era. The systemic move towards disintermediation, and having others act on our behalf under the guise of collectivised economies of scale, now sits at the philosophical heart of modern society. Take pension investing, for example, which for a lot of developed economies is now enforced via opt-out schemes for employees, which has both artificially inflated the role of institutional investors upon modern society, but also changed how the economy must be managed. Poor decision-making from a pension fund could have dire consequences for large parts of a given society. However, it is more existential than this, and with the rise of the so-called 'universal owner', so-called because there are institutional investors like BlackRock or Vanguard that hold so many assets across different asset classes that (a) divesting from one sector will usually hurt it in another, and (b) they are blowing apart traditional understandings of the governance of companies that is focused on the role and predilections of the 'shareholder'. The concepts of liability, signalling, and the role of ESG rating agencies are all fundamentally intertwined with this particular dynamic, as we shall continue to see.

Yet, seeking to positively affect informational asymmetries cannot just be done by focusing on institutional investors alone, however influential they may be. What really needs to be the focus is the entire informational flow within the modern economy, and to that end the EU turned their attention to the role that companies play in injecting the right amount and types of information into the economic ecosystem. The NFRD, as mentioned above, sought to improve the information being provided by large companies within the EU (those with over 500 employees). However, as I said just above, the EU has a particular composition that means that focusing on large entities probably will not allow for an adequate amount of information to be injected into the European economic machine. So, to remedy this the EU has recently launched the latest component of their Action Plan: the CSRD, or the Corporate Sustainability Reporting Directive. The CSRD seeks to build upon the foundation developed by the NFRD and instead now aims at a larger audience, as the European Commission explains:

> On 5 January 2023, the Corporate Sustainability Reporting Directive (CSRD) entered into force. This new directive modernises and strengthens the rules concerning the social and environmental information that companies have to report. A broader set of large companies, as well as listed SMEs, will now be required to report on sustainability – approximately 50,000 companies in total.[18]

The Commission goes on to explain that the CSRD will produce more transparency by mandating disclosures on a range of sustainability topics, but that this disclosure will also be enhanced by mandating that it is all done against the 'European Sustainability Reporting Standards (ESRS)', which were developed by the European Financial Reporting Advisory Group (EFRAG), an independent body that built the standards by combining the influence of numerous stakeholders and aligning everything to stated EU policies. In addition, the information provided by companies against the CSRD framework needs to be audited and digitalised, to further aid with the objectives of improving transparency across the bloc. Under the Directive, the Commission 'must adopt legislation to provide for limited assurance standards (by 1 October 2026), as well as further legislation to provide for reasonable assurance standards (by 1 October 2028)'.[19]

The CSRD will be difficult to transition to, mostly because it now aims to encompass various SMEs to better represent the picture of the European marketplace.[20] Furthermore, the CSRD applies to large listed and now unlisted companies as well, which also includes listed micro-companies as well as the EU subsidiaries of non-EU parent companies.[21] The Commission has also detailed a timeline for transitioning to the CSRD, with companies already subject to the NFRD needing to comply with the CSRD from FY2024, followed by FY2025 for large companies not already subject to the NFRD, and FY2026 for listed SMEs. For the non-EU companies with EU subsidiaries, FY2028 has been put forward as the date at which they will have to start complying with the CSRD's disclosure requirements. The data that these entities will have to disclose is also much more complex than that of the NFRD, with firms needing to include Scope 3 emission data across their supply chains. Also, in addition to needing independent verification and assurance of the disclosures made, the company's information that it discloses will need to be included in the directors' reports, essentially 'making Directors responsible in writing for ESG performance'.[22]

This hugely complex undertaking has already revealed intrinsic difficulties. The most obvious so far is that the aim to simplify things for companies, in terms of regulatory disclosure-related requirements, has not been achieved quite simply because the EU is acting in the EU's interest (as is its prerogative). This is witnessed when analysing the recently revealed and long-awaited 'Sustainability Disclosure Standards' from the International Sustainability Standards Board (ISSB), housed within the International Financial Reporting Standards (IFRS) body. Those standards have chosen to focus on what is known as 'single materiality', or more simply, the effect of sustainability issues on the financial performance of a company. The CSRD instead focuses on 'double materiality' which describes the notion above, but with the added focus of the impact of the company upon the environment around it. This disparity has been noted early by onlookers who have preliminarily analysed the transaction costs for those mandated to disclose.[23]

The reality is that, as Moloney says, the EU currently has the highest standards regarding sustainability disclosure anywhere in the world. On the face of it this is a positive thing for the European experience moving forward, but in the short term it presents tremendous difficulties, as others may not be obliged to follow the Europeans' lead. Furthermore, the culture of other jurisdictions may simply not allow for developments like that witnessed across the European bloc, and that seems to be the case when the developments in other jurisdictions are assessed. To demonstrate this, the development within the US is a good case study for how differing cultures and relationships with business can impact upon the direction and trajectory of travel in the sustainability space.

In the US, the development of a systemic focus on sustainability has simply not been possible. The swings of the American electorate, from the Obama administration to the Trump administration, and then to the Biden administration, has made the task difficult, but this is all against a backdrop of congressional division that makes any such approach to alter the systematic consideration of how business should normatively operate almost impossible to consider. Nevertheless, there have been some substantial developments recently. In 2022, the US Securities and Exchange Commission (SEC) announced a proposed rule that would force about 6,000 corporate entities to include within their financial statement an assessment of climate risks associated with their operations, and also how they are managing such identified risks.[24] In addition to this, the proposal dictates that an 'attestation report' would also need to be filed from an independent service provider who could verify details relating to Scope 1 and Scope 2 emission claims. Scope 3 claims would also need to be covered, if they were deemed to be material to the company or the firm has established a particular target or goal related to reducing Scope 3 emissions.

The SEC's efforts came on the back of substantial pressure from institutional investors seeking more and better-quality information, as well as its own concerns about the rise of greenwashing within the US financial space.[25] The proposed rule is a direct reaction to the climate risk framework developed by the Task Force on Climate-Related Financial Disclosures (TCFD). However, there has been concern raised by market participants regarding what is seen as an overly ambitious timescale, with large entities to begin reporting in FY2023, and smaller companies in FY2024 and FY2025 depending on size.

The proposed rule by the SEC has still not been finalised at the time of writing (mid-2023), and the uncertainty about what the rule will look like is spawning a market in itself for advice, consultancy, and support for those that will be affected. However, whilst the rule is a reaction to international standard-setting, the foundation for the legal consideration of ESG within the US is fraught with complexity. Any crime or misdeed relating to financial matters in the US is usually dealt with by rules surrounding disclosure, which Nelson suggests will become even more problematic as the concept of ESG becomes more mainstream: 'an important reason why the line between civil and criminal culpability for fraud is likely to blur regarding ESG is that there is so much economic pressure on companies to assert their role in this area to investors. There is money to be made from saying what investors want to hear, even if it is not true.'[26]

The legal focus on disclosure in the US is growing. Hackett et al. discuss how even though claims relating to sustainability in the US have often focused on package labelling, more cases are coming through relating to statements made in relation to ESG performance and capabilities. As the scholars note, 'While these claims have been largely unsuccessful to date in achieving significant changes in company ESG reporting, plaintiffs have made notable progress with a growing number of courts allowing cases to proceed beyond the motion to dismiss stage, where the threat of discovery has prompted settlements and course corrections.'[27] This has led onlookers to suggest that the potential threats to companies making ESG-related disclosures are counterproductive, and result in a concept known as 'green-hushing' – where entities will refuse to disclose their ESG performance, even if it is positive, for fear of being exposed to undue liability. To remedy this, onlookers have been calling for 'safe harbours' to be set up by the SEC in order to allow issuers to be more transparent and induce dialogue between the issuers and the market, without necessarily having the threat of liability imposed.[28]

In the US courts, the question of disclosure has usually led to the question of what may be 'material' information. For example, Anderson discusses how the courts have usually delineated between 'hard' information and 'soft' information, with hard information being that which is 'typically historical information or other factual information that is objectively verifiable'. Soft information, on the other hand, includes 'predictions and matters of opinion and is only actionable if it is virtually as certain as hard facts'. The implication of this for ESG-related disclosure is that 'misstatements that consist of vague, aspirational statements or statements of policy and values are generally not considered material' with an important fact of the courts being that 'this materiality framework is independent of the subject of the statement'. For statements or disclosures to be held as material, there is somewhat of a checklist that courts follow that includes such elements as whether the misstatement arises from an item capable of precise measurement or whether it arises from an estimate. This leads Anderson to question whether 'ESG statements can ever be qualitatively material because they do not directly impact a company's profitability'. Yet, Anderson counteracts this understanding, saying that as a lot of ESG-related disclosure is backward-looking, it can be measured and therefore becomes precise enough to be counted as material under the courts' own parameters.[29]

Ultimately, as Kuratek et al. note, the reality is that the landscape for liability exposure in relation to ESG information in the US is changing. Most of the disclosure-related claims are captured under Section 11 of the Securities Act of 1933, which focuses on material misstatements and omissions in securities offerings documents, but also other anti-fraud legal rulings that extend to less formal communications like reports, press releases, and websites.[30] Once we add to this the understanding that the SEC's proposed rule will move the US needle towards mandating disclosure on particular issues, the writing may be on the wall for American corporate entities in relation to ESG-related disclosure. Yet, the story will likely not be a straightforward one. The cultural 'battle' being waged in the US between political ends of the spectrum in relation to 'woke' culture is spilling over into the financial sector at a rapid rate. Several states have banned their institutional investors from considering non-financial information and threatened increased liability for those that do so, whilst several companies have lost billions of dollars overnight for selling products that have been perceived to be 'woke' (see the case of Bud Light in 2023). With the US election due in November 2024, the pendulum could swing either way and reset the boundaries once more, which in reality is not what the investment community needs at all. The movement of ESG in the American context is complicated, complex, and certainly not certain.

The realm of disclosure is clearly one of the instrumental pillars to making the financial sector more sustainable in the long run. Determining how companies and investors are considering such issues, how they are integrating them into the practices, and also how they are preparing for their effects is all crucial information. That level of information stands a chance of breaking down some of the key informational asymmetries that are witnessed in the field with regards to the relationship between 'business' and the environment around it. However, it is not the only pillar. Understanding the modern concept of 'business' brings us directly to the concept of the principal–agent relationship and also the concept of directors having particular duties to their companies. These issues are critical in understanding the relationship between 'business' and the environment around it, so we shall now look to consider those issues in more detail.

3.   THE PRINCIPAL–AGENT RELATIONSHIP

As just a small interlude for our progression, it would be useful to understand what is meant by the concepts of 'principals' and 'agents', and the relationship that exists between them. This book is concerned with the prospective role of the ESG rating agencies, and to understand that dynamic as best as we can, some deconstruction is needed. At the risk of becoming too existential, the role of ESG rating agencies is a microcosm of a much larger and systemic dynamic that is fundamentally intertwined with facets of human behaviour and psychology, social ordering, and capitalism in its conceptual form. A better understanding of what is known as 'agency theory' reveals these foundational aspects upon which we can understand ESG ratings better.

Delbufalo tells that the modern concept of 'agency theory' largely originates from the works of Mitnick, Ross, and in the management literature from Eisenhardt, and Jensen and Meckling.[31] Brandsma and Adriaensen's simple definition of the theory is that 'the principal, primarily motivated by efficiency reasons, chooses to delegate power to an agent. In return, the principal can control the powers of the agent.'[32] The necessary context for this conceptualisation is perhaps found in the form of the concept of 'separation of ownership' popularised by Berle and Means in their 1932 work.[33] The concept of separation of ownership is intrinsically linked to the modern form of capitalism, as Pacces discusses:

> Economic theory of corporate governance approaches separation of ownership and control as a problem of separation of firm management from firm finance... Managers and financiers of course need each other. A manager (or an entrepreneur) 'needs the financiers' funds, wince he either does not have enough capital of his own to invest or else wants to cash out his holdings'. However, the focus of the corporate governance debate is rather on how managers are hired by financiers, and on what terms. As a result, no different from other long-term contractual relations, corporate governance is typically regarded as an agency problem: financiers act as the principals, hiring one or more agents to generate returns on their funds.
>
> In this perspective, the manager's position might look not much different from that of a high-rank employee. However, what distinguishes managers from the rest of the company's employees is their position on top of the firm hierarchy. Corporate managers are vested with enormous discretionary powers, for they bear ultimate

responsibility of how the firm is managed. This discretion is the very essence of firm control.[34]

The importance of the 'agent' is clear. In a modern decentralised firm, the shareholders of the company are the 'residual claimants on the firm's assets', but as they tend to lack 'both coordination and the necessary expertise, they do not know how to manage them in such a way as to maximise their value as an open-ended stream of profits'.[35] Even if there is some modicum of expertise and willingness to coordinate amongst shareholders, growth and the potential of bringing in more shareholders fundamentally dilutes the options of the shareholders. In the modern capitalistic era, the globalised nature of investing, which can take the form of investing in companies via shares and not debt, means the willingness and capability of shareholders to manage the companies they own is zero.

This constantly shifting power dynamic is, however, also a very human story. Whilst companies as legal entities may be shareholders, to manage a firm will always (for the time being at least) be a distinctly human endeavour, which brings with it connected problems and opportunities. As Delbufalo alluded to earlier, agency theory has tended to apply categorised understandings of 'actors' within its definition of the 'agency problem', as Jensen and Meckling illustrate in their seminal 1976 work *Theory of the Firm*:

> We define an agency relationship as a contract under which one or more persons (the principal(s)) engage another person (the agent) to perform some service on their behalf which involves delegating some decision-making authority to the agent. If both parties to the relationship are utility maximizers there is good reason to believe that the agent will not always act in the best interests of the principal. The principal can limit divergences from his interest by establishing appropriate incentives for the agent and by incurring monitoring costs designed to limit the aberrant activities, of the agent. In addition in some situations it will pay the agent to expend resources (bonding costs) to guarantee that he will not take certain actions which would harm the principal or to ensure that the principal will be compensated if he does take such actions. However, it is generally impossible for the principal or the agent at zero cost to ensure that the agent will make optimal decisions from the principal's viewpoint.[36]

The scholars suggest that the associated costs for this relationship come via the monitoring expenditures of the principal, the bonding expenditures of the agent, and the residual loss associated with the whole process.

It is worth noting that this phenomenon is not exclusive to the financial sector. As Jensen and Meckling make clear, 'it exists in all organisations and in all cooperative efforts'. That generality has allowed researchers to better understand the underlying dynamics. Both Brandsma and Adriaensen, and Delbufalo discuss the fact that within the agency theory parameters, the principal is superior. The former illustrates that one line of thinking suggests that the 'principal's preferences should always prevail and the agent must follow these slavishly', whilst the latter suggest that agency theory is all geared to view the relationship from the perspective of the principal, not the agent, and thus demonstrating their superiority. As Delbufalo indicates, 'an efficient contract is "one that brings about the best possible outcome for the principal given the constraints imposed by the situation, rather than one that maximises the joint utility of both principal and agent"'.[37] However, whilst an agent may need to follow the principal's wishes slavishly in the realm of, say, representative democracy, it is more than questionable whether that is true for the business arena (and it is questionable whether the same is true within a representative democracy really).

Hart states that instead of the manager being an entity devoid of emotions like self-interest, ambition, and other aspects which may affect their duty, they instead may be interested in goals that go beyond simply maximising the welfare of the owners. Additionally, he notes that the manager's actions, like how hard they work, is only really observable to the manager themselves. Furthermore, the manager has the best position to the see the profitability of the firm, so attempting to bind the actions of the agent or incentivise them via financial reward linked to the profitability of the company may not be as effective as it may seem. Perhaps more foundationally, Hart says that 'even under an optimal incentive scheme, however, the manager will put some weight on his own objectives at the expense of the owners (unless he is risk-neutral and wealthy, in which case the owners will sell the firm to him)'.[38] In a round-about way, this reveals that there is conflict inherent within the relationship between principal and agent. Thirion et al. discuss how, in order to alleviate this conflict, rewards are often offered to align more the positions of the two entities. However, tying rewards to performance where effort cannot be directly observed has the potential to lead to perverse outcomes:

> although the long-standing agency theory prescription has been to condition variable compensation solely on profits and other financial accounting figures, recent literature has criticized this approach, suggesting that it encourages managers to sacrifice long-run firm performance to increase short-term financial results in an effort to maximize the agent's personal compensation.[39]

It is not hard to contextualise this within the GFC that had short-termism and perverse incentivisation at its very core.

Ultimately, the agency problem is important for our understanding of ESG rating agencies, as the book will make clear as it progresses. For the relationship between the law and ESG as a concept, it is clear that agency issues are vitally important. This is mostly because of the subjective nature of

ESG-related considerations, in direct association with the importance of them. Everything comes down to the core interests and motivations of the owners of property. For instance, if a company's shareholders have very little interest in the running of the company and are merely focused on shareholding value and dividends, then why would an agent focus on anything other than the financial health of the company? One may argue that they ought to focus on numerous non-financial elements because they *can* play a role in the financial health of the company, but critics of this argument suggest that if those aspects are *material*, the agent will already be considering them because their sole interest is on the financial health of the company. However, this is complicated when we change the language, and instead suggest that the shareholders are mostly (or only) interested in profit maximisation. If an agent is then only interested in profit maximisation *and* their personal compensation is tied to short-term goals, considering non-financial information which *may* be material at some point automatically carries less weight.

There is of course a balance to this slightly cynical view of the world, one which sees the agents become *stewards*. This concept is very much encouraged within the realm of institutional investing, with many signing up to so-called stewardship codes around the world that push for agents to demonstrate sound, forward-looking and responsible principles in their decision-making processes.[40] Yet, this is certainly not the norm within the financial sector. Therefore, with the rise of ESG and non-financial information flooding the modern business environment, the principal–agent dynamic is needing to undergo dramatic changes to cope with new pressures. One pressure that has always existed in relation to the principal–agent dynamic and which is only becoming more acute is that of a director, as having ultimate responsibility for the company, being exposed to liability because of this new environment.

4.   KEY LEGAL CONSIDERATIONS: DUTY

The duties that the agent owes to the principal are sacrosanct within the concept of a company. The law has grown to codify such duties so that companies may be protected from human interference, with intention being a low bar on many occasions. The concepts of 'trust' within a legal framework, and then when applied to financial matters, differs around the world but has central tenets running throughout, which we will assess now in this section. Whilst a lot of this section's focus will be on what is known as 'directors' duties', those are not the only times when a so-called *fiduciary* relationship exists. Many agents will have not only contractually agreed upon duties to their principals, but fiduciary duties in the eyes of the law. Yet, the easiest example for our understanding will be found when analysing the role, position, responsibilities, and limitations of directors.

Perhaps one of the most pressing questions of our time, at least with regards to the intersection of ESG and business, has always been whether including anything other than hard, verifiable, and quantitative financial data will expose a director or manager to liability. In fact, the debate has often strayed into the realms of whether directors and managers are even technically able to consider non-financial information in their deliberations. A relatively early answer, which we shall look at now, came to the conclusion that not only were agents able and technically allowed to consider non-financial information, not doing so would potentially put them in breach of their legal and contractual duties. That pinnacle understanding has been built upon since, although the environment around the world of ESG consideration and integration, particularly in terms of politics within developed economies, has fundamentally changed and continues to shift.

In the years after the turn of the millennium, the United Nations Environment Programme Finance Initiative (UNEP-FI) had been working on better understanding the intersection between investment and the environment within which it takes place. A division of UNEP-FI asked a bespoke team of specialist lawyers at Freshfields Bruckhaus Deringer, led by Professor Paul Watchman, to investigate this issue from within the legal perspective and answer the following question:

> Is the integration of environmental, social and governance issues into investment policy (including asset allocation, portfolio construction and stock-picking or bond-picking) voluntarily permitted, legally required or hampered by law and regulation; primarily as regards public and private pension funds, secondarily as regards insurance company reserves and mutual funds?[41]

In seeking to provide an answer to that question, the team would provide one of the most accessed UN reports in the UN's history, perhaps indicating the central importance of the question in and of itself, and the answer.

In relation to investment decision-makers in particular, the report discusses how, within common-law-focused jurisdictions, 'fiduciary duties are the key source of limits on the discretion of investment decision-makers... the most important fiduciary duties are the duty to act prudently and the duty to act in accordance with the purpose for which investment powers are granted (also known as the duty of loyalty)'. The report goes on to say:

> Broadly, fiduciary duties are duties imposed upon a person who exercises some discretionary power in the interests of another person in circumstances that give rise to a relationship of trust and confidence. Fiduciary duties are largely a product of case law. As common law jurisdictions often look to case law from other common law jurisdictions to inform their own law, there is a considerable degree of overlap in the law of fiduciary duties between these jurisdictions.

However, even though common law jurisdictions have advanced the issue of integrating non-financial information into business processes, the UK serves as a good example of how far there is still to go. The majority of the duties of directors are housed within the Companies Act 2006, sections 170 to 181. The main bulk of the duties are as to be expected, ranging from a director having a duty to promote the success of the company, to exercise independent judgement, to exercise reasonable care, skill, and diligence, to avoid conflicts of interests, and to declare interests in proposed transactions or arrangements. The sentiment is a simple one: the agent should be operating to promote the principal, which in the director's case is the company.

However, as a slight aside from the main analysis in this section, recent developments have put the accepted frameworks under strain. Just one of the ways in which directors can be held accountable is via a mechanism called a derivative action. A derivative action entails a shareholder petitioning the court to take action on behalf of the company when it is shown that a reasonable director would have done so – the implication being that the director or directors in charge are not acting in the company's best interests and would have taken different actions were they doing so. If the courts agree with the claim of the shareholder, and there is usually a series of tests and bars for the claim to pass before that happens, then the court will take charge of the company under the relevant statute for the purposes of remedying the harm caused by the directors in that instance. That is dealt with via sections 260 to 269 in the Companies Act. Theoretically, any shareholder may bring such a claim and, interestingly, this is precisely what has been happening at the very largest of companies involved in extractive practices recently, with Shell being a prime example. Activists who take positions in such companies, like 'ClientEarth', who pursue legal action on behalf of the planet, have initiated internal legal actions against directors for breaching their duties because of strategies that involve the continuation of oil and gas extraction.[42] However, such instances are being challenged because it is being alleged that the actions are not being brought in the company's best interests, but because of an agenda held by the shareholder. As a result, the law is in stasis in the UK as the courts and the government decide the best way forward. The UK government is currently reviewing the rules around pension trustees' fiduciary duties in order to clarify the 'latitude' of fiduciary duties in relation to apparently systematic targets of net zero and broad sustainability and stewardship initiatives.[43] It has been suggested elsewhere that progression in the Shell case could have an immediate impact elsewhere in the world, especially in the US, which has taken a particular route with regards to answering this question, as we shall see shortly.[44]

Returning to our journey through the so-called Freshfields Report, the report states:

> Civil law jurisdictions do not recognise fiduciary duties as such, those duties being a product of the common law. However, investment decision-makers in these jurisdictions are subject to obligations that in many circumstances give rise to equivalent duties. These obligations are articulated in various statutory provisions regulating the conduct of investment decision-makers and in the government and other guidelines that assist in the interpretation of these provisions.

The report found that, in reality, the difference between common law and civil law jurisdictional understandings is merely form, not substance. Both formats have the same core principles revolving around the concepts of processes, loyalty, and pursuing proper objectives. This is all rational given what we understand about the principal–agent dynamic. Whilst it is acknowledged that this analysis is flitting between investment managers and directors, which have different responsibilities, they share core responsibilities that apply across the board from within the principal–agent dynamic.

In terms of how the law approaches this issue of integrating ESG considerations into everyday business practices more generally, the trend is not really going in one concerted direction. For example, Turner discusses how the UK was seen to take the lead with its 2006 Companies Act, which moved the dial on what is known as 'stakeholder theory' (namely that a company owes duties to more than just the shareholders). Canada and France have also been noted as developing their law to move in the same direction.[45] However, Turner describes these types of endeavours as 'legal construct initiatives' as they seek to impact the fiduciary duties of directors. Yet, in a more existential sense, Turner discusses how the reality is that no government, anywhere, has sought to infringe on the tripartite that makes up the modern company: 'separate legal personality', 'limited liability', and 'fiduciary duties'. These elements are sacrosanct apparently, and changing them could have massive consequences; Turner muses that 'lessons from the past demonstrate that individual countries will ultimately be unwilling to adopt law that places those businesses incorporated under their jurisdiction at a competitive disadvantage. Therefore if significant steps in this regard are to take place it would require a high degree of international consensus.' Citing Sjafjell, he continues by saying:

> while company law will not solve all the problems, it is a missing piece of the sustainability puzzle that needs to be put in its place. It is also a piece that has tended to be ignored in the debate on how to encourage companies to behave in an environmentally and socially friendly manner.[46]

In line with the seminal findings of the Freshfields Report, scholars have since been seeking to understand better the conditions under which directors' actions will not be deemed to have breached any fiduciary duties. This is important because in furtherance of the question of whether a director should take ESG considerations into account or not, the next stage is to ask what may be the consequence for them doing so? If a director does take into account particular non-financial information, and then the company performs poorly, will they be liable? It would be a rare instance if a company director or investment manager was to integrate non-financial ESG-related information, perform well, and then still face claims that could lead to them being found to be liable. To answer this developed question, we need to return to the concept of there being an informational flow through the business.

Speaking from an American perspective, although it is representative of corporate law around the world, Lipton confirms that:

> In carrying out decision-making, corporate law imposes on boards a fiduciary duty of care to act on a reasonably informed basis after due consideration of relevant information and appropriate deliberation. This means that directors must take actions necessary to assure themselves that they have the information required to take, or refrain from taking, action; that they devote sufficient time to the consideration of such information; and that they obtain, where helpful, advice from appropriate experts.[47]

Lipton continues by stating:

> By ignoring or not taking into account the interests of stakeholders and ESG considerations, a corporation will not be able to sustain itself over the long term. Considering the interests of not only shareholders, but also all who are critical to the success of the company, is essential to ensuring long-term sustainability, and is consistent with the board's fiduciary obligation to inform itself of and consider all relevant information. To be sure, Delaware courts have long recognized and accepted that, outside of the context of a change-of-control transaction, corporate boards can and should take into account the interests of all relevant stakeholders in pursuing long-term value for the corporation. Doing so is consistent with the fiduciary duty of care, as well as with the board's obligation under the Caremark doctrine to implement and monitor systems to identify material risks, and to address risks once identified.[48]

Whilst we will cover the *Caremark* case that Lipton refers to above shortly, the sentiment here is clear. Not only is considering ESG acceptable in the eyes of the law, but not doing so may find you liable. This is in line with the Freshfield Report. However, what the law is adding is a clear condition that has clear ramifications for this book: a director must be able to 'show their workings' when considering non-financial information, and they must do this by outsourcing some of the due diligence to perceived or accepted 'experts' who can inject specialised information into the decision-making process. Speaking in relation to an important Australian case (*ASIC v. Avestra*), Pamela Hanrahan confirmed:

> This means that the director will be taken to have discharged their duty to act with care and diligence if they can establish that they made the judgment in good faith for a proper purpose; did not have a material personal interest in the subject matter of the judgment; *informed themselves about the subject matter of the judgment to the extent they reasonably believe to be appropriate*; and rationally believe that the judgment is in the best interests of the corporation. The director's belief that the judgment is in the best interests of the corporation is a rational one unless the belief is one that no reasonable person in their position would hold.[49]

This is a legal approach that is demonstrated around the world. Ferreira and Sequeira discuss how this could be related to a concept known in the US as the 'business judgment rule'. This rule describes the limitation acknowledged by the courts on their own reach, based in the understanding that (i) judges do not have the means (including the technical expertise) to review the merits of a director's decisions *ex post*, (ii) there are no objective rules for management, and (iii) due to the absence of clear standards 'hindsight bias (with information collected subsequently) "can make even the most reasonable managerial decision seem reckless *ex post*"'. The scholars discuss how it is accepted that risk-taking is a crucial foundational element of business and that losses cannot be removed from the scope of doing business.[50] The scholars do, however, acknowledge that the application of this rule will differ between jurisdictions and, in the case of multi-state federal jurisdictions like the US, differ state to state. This is perhaps emblematic of the constant existence of cultural factors affecting the act of constraining and overseeing the act of conducting business.

In the US, one particular case was heard that, initially, was written off as being too problematic to change the course of the law in any significant way. Yet, recent decisions have fundamentally changed that course, and the *Re Caremark International Inc. Derivative Litigation* case, more commonly referred to simply as *Caremark*, has become centrally important to the direction of corporate duties in the US. Shapira neatly summarises the details and effect of the case:

> The 1996 Caremark decision changed corporate law's approach to board oversight duties, from reactive to proactive. Prior to Caremark, directors could assume that everything was fine until someone in the company flagged a problem to them. Caremark introduced a duty to implement a system that tracks and reports potential problems to the board, and to constantly monitor that system and to react to the red flags that it raises. At the same time, Caremark called on judges to show restraint, and impose liability only when it is clear that directors knew they were breach-

ing their duties. Negligence or even gross negligence is not enough; to establish a Caremark claim, plaintiffs have to show bad faith on the part of the directors.

The bad-faith requirement turned into an insuperable pleading hurdle. Plaintiffs had to plead with particularity facts about what directors knew and when they knew it, which is not the type of evidence that one can glean from public documents and without access to discovery. As a result, plaintiffs usually resorted to regurgitating facts about the trauma that the company suffered, but did not (could not) link the trauma to bad faith on the part of the directors. Caremark lawsuits then turned into a parade of early dismissals, and corporate legal scholars were denouncing Caremark as a 'toothless tiger'.[51]

The facts of the case centred around a derivative claim that stated that the board had breached their duty of care by failing to establish adequate control systems, with the result being criminal offences taking place which cost the company more than $250 million in fines and civil penalties. The judge ruling found that the board can be seen to have met its standards of duty if it actively seeks to adequately inform itself of any issues that relate to its mandate, and act accordingly. Again, the informational flow comes to the fore.

However, in 2019, a case was brought under the *Caremark* precedent that sought to really put the application of the precedent under review. The *Marchand v. Barnhill* case, commonly referred to as the Blue Bell case, consisted of a claim brought against the Blue Bell Creameries ice cream manufacturer, who had suffered a listeria outbreak in 2015 and was subsequently forced into a massive recall and shutdown. The inability to contain the outbreak led to the deaths of three people, and ultimately a liquidity crisis that forced the company into a dilutive private equity arrangement. A shareholder brought the derivative claim against two key executives and claimed that they had breached their duties by knowingly disregarding contamination risks and failing to oversee the food-making operations of the company adequately enough.

The Court of Chancery, at first instance, routinely dismissed the claim because of the lack of a 'smoking gun' indication that the executives knew about the issues and ignored them. Proving state of mind in this instance clearly is a high bar, and is one of the criticisms of the *Caremark* case. Yet, upon appeal, the Delaware Supreme Court ruled that the lack of indication that the board had even discussed the food safety problems was itself an indication that the board had failed in their duty. As Shapira explains:

> If you are a director of a company that sells only ice cream, and you do not ensure that the board regularly discusses food safety issues, you are probably not making a good-faith effort to engage in oversight, the court reasoned. Importantly, the court identified food safety as 'mission critical' for an ice-cream manufacturing company, and implied that board oversight of such critical issues is subject to heightened judicial scrutiny.[52]

Legal scholars then wondered whether the *Marchand* case would become the new standard, and almost immediately they go their answer. Three cases using the *Caremark* precedent survived motions to appeal, meaning that *Marchand* was not unique because it led to deaths, and that it had developed the law so that the nature of the business and what was seen to be critical was now also of importance when deciding whether a director should have acted or not. Shapira explains that this new era of judicial reasoning in the US rests on two particular pillars: an increased willingness to apply heightened scrutiny of board oversight via the 'mission critical' designation, and also an increased willingness to grant outside shareholders access to internal company documents, in order to investigate potential failure of oversight claims. A perfect example of this new era was seen in the Boeing cases in the wake of the two tragic crashes of the new Max-8 aircrafts: *Caremark* cases survived early motions to dismiss based upon the new pillars of reasoning. The Boeing case, however, changes the nature of the new post-*Caremark* era because the sheer size and complexity of Boeing means the reach of the precedent has grown. As Shapira concludes:

> The courts now order provision of documents in more cases, and order provision of more types of documents. In that respect, footnote 1 may be the most important part of the Boeing decision: it tells us that prior to filing the derivative action, plaintiffs submitted a request to inspect the company's books and records, which gave them access to 630,000 pages of internal Boeing materials relevant to airplane safety oversight. Giving sophisticated plaintiffs access to 630,000 pages of internal discussions completely alters the prospect of Caremark liability. Armed with this powerful pre-suit discovery tool, plaintiffs have strong chances of finding indications of one of two alternative Caremark prongs: (1) that directors utterly failed to collect information about a critical issue, or (2) that directors collected information but failed to respond to red flags.[53]

There have been more cases since, like that of Marriott Hotels, who suffered a catastrophic data breach. What this development in the case law tells us is fascinating and leads us directly into the next chapter.

Ultimately, the days of checking boxes and moving on are over. The pressure on directors is now acute in particular areas of their business.[54] It is no longer enough to casually consider something because if, after the fact, it is found to be centrally important for your business or, in other words, 'mission critical', not considering it fully and obtaining the necessary expertise to understand it can be costly. Strine et al. discuss how recent cases have confirmed that directors may be held liable if they do not take active steps to ensure that the information flow up to them is adequate enough, and that this must be demonstrable upon inspection.[55] The scholars note how law firms are actively advising boards of directors of this need to demonstrate thinking *ex post*, with corporate boards now desperate to find ways of not only implementing good ESG practices in their business, but also being able to demonstrate it. What they are crying out for is a *signal*.

It is on that note that we move into the next chapter. Hopefully, I have indicated slightly enough throughout the book so far small titbits that are accumulating as we go through. The informational flows that are critical within the modern business environment do not just exist in one dimension. The informational flow is multidimensional, and the need to signal is fundamentally attached to that informational flow. For example, and to foreshadow a discussion later in the book, what may be a good way for those desperate boards to *signal* that they considered ESG issues affecting their business? Well, first they have to know and be able to show that they sought to learn what was material, and then they have to show that they engaged with experts to learn more about the potential impact of those issues. What industry theoretically exists to provide both rankings of ESG issues and complementary ancillary/ consultative service that can guide you through the process? You can see why any inefficiencies in the ESG rating space could cause havoc, systemically. In the next chapter we will see that there are certainly inefficiencies at present and that, currently, regulators around the world are breaking their necks to try to resolve them so that the facilitative nature of a functioning ratings industry can be applied to these myriad requirements we have only touched the surface of in this chapter.

5.   CONCLUSION

This chapter has sought to better understand the intersection between the law's understanding of ESG, and its application within the business arena. One of the clear conclusions that we must draw from the chapter's analysis is that, unsurprisingly, the issue is tremendously multifaceted. As a result, a variety of legal mechanisms are being employed to bring order to the new era of business that itself was a response to the height of degenerative standards within the business realm. ESG, as a clear reaction to the system that allowed for the GFC, brings with it exceptional opportunities but intrinsic weaknesses that reveal themselves when the concept is applied to human culture.

The chapter examined the key pillars of the intersection and focused on the areas of disclosure and duty. In the area of disclosure, we saw that the EU has taken strides ahead of its peers in establishing systemic changes to tackle the issue of sustainability. However, not without issue, the EU is currently fighting to apply its sector-leading rulings into workable frameworks that business, and crucially international business, can abide by. Yet, it has been insistent on high standards that take into account the European experience, and initiatives like the SFDR are now being supplemented by the incredibly ambitious and potentially very impactful CSRD, which brings on board the SMEs that make up the majority of European businesses. As other jurisdictions race to form their own versions of the same initiatives, like the US's focus on climate disclosure mainly, it is clear that it is widely acknowledged that if corporate culture is going to change, the informational flow is what will need to be adapted.

That informational flow is a key element to the whole concept of corporate bodies. Something which is equally as critical is the concept of the principal–agent relationship, and in this chapter we were introduced to agency theory, which seeks to describe the underlying power dynamics in a decentralised entity. Focusing on the corporate sector, we saw how principals need to both restrain the actions of the agents they select to actually run their businesses with the necessary expertise, but also incentivise them so that operational objectives that benefit the principal are met. Again, the informational flow between the two parties here is crucial, as is the need to communicate in a manner that is appropriate, informational enough, and also efficient. Again, ESG ratings as a concept was alluded to ahead of analyses coming next in the book.

In a more punitive tone, the chapter then considered the concept of directors and managers as having *duties*. The concept of one having fiduciary duties was analysed to examine the importance of the informational flow and the multidimensionality of it as it applied to various scenarios and levels of responsibility. Via case law in the United States, it became clear that ESG as a corporate consideration is becoming the norm and that the legal architecture is slowly recognising this fact. However, what was more important is that diverting one's attention away from traditional metrics in any way required 'cookie crumbs' that could be investigated after the fact, something which is even more important when we consider the subjective nature of ESG as a concept.

Throughout the whole chapter the concepts of information and signalling were under the surface. This is because they are conceptually attached to the concept of modern business. However, it is worth discussing something here as we conclude the chapter that must not be forgotten, as Turner indicates as he talks of his own article on the subject:

> What this article also demonstrates is that there is a broader long-term case for reconsidering the design of the legal construct of the company itself. The existing design has been extremely successful over the last 220 years in providing a medium for businesses to attract and maintain investment. However, it has been less successful in terms of the impacts that companies have had on peoples' human rights and the environment. The article has demonstrated that a redesign of the corporation as a legal construct requires a process that takes into account all aspects of its key components rather than isolating and solely focusing upon directors' duties. What is also clear is that whatever re-design or new framework might be envisaged for the future, it would need to incorporate mechanisms that would ultimately continue to encourage investors and protect their interests if the corporation is to continue to be successful as a medium for business in free market economies.[56]

The company is still the premium model of development within the capitalistic mode of society. It is synonymous with the concept of capitalism, and seeking to amend it will cause huge controversy. It is instructive that despite all of the revolutionary reforms under the guise of sustainability, the reality is that the key fundamental aspects of the company – separate legal personality, limited liability, and fiduciary duties – have remained entirely untouched.

There is a message we can take from this. Whilst sustainability concerns will hopefully move business into a state of being less extractive, less destructive, and more positive for the human race's relationship with the planet, the reality is that there must be benefit for those in the company. Affecting the flexibility and potential to create and withdraw profit must not be interfered with, many will say. If that is the case, there are direct implications for ESG rating agencies. There are clearly multidimensional roles that the ESG ratings must fill, but to do so they must be one thing: facilitative. To be facilitative means to be useful to the corporate infrastructure and the modality of capitalism. The rewards for doing so could be astronomical – it is not surprising to know now that the credit rating agencies are amongst the most profitable companies, in terms of ratio, on the planet – but one *must* be geared towards being systemically facilitative. The question now for the ESG rating space is whether there is enough to suggest that they have the capability to meet that demand.

NOTES

1. Pedro Matos, *ESG and Responsible Institutional Investing Around the World: A Critical Review* (CFA 2020) 15.
2. MSCI, *What is ESG?* (2023) https://www.msci.com/esg-101-what-is-esg.
3. PRI, *What is ESG Integration?* (2023) https://www.unpri.org/investment-tools/what-is-esg-integration/3052.article.
4. John Hill, *Environmental, Social, and Governance (ESG) Investing: A Balanced Analysis of the Theory and Practice of a Sustainable Portfolio* (Elsevier 2020) 13.
5. Hiroki Sampei, 'ESG awareness is an enduring legacy of the global financial crisis' (2018) Fidelity International (Sept 12) https://www.fidelityinternational .com/ editorial/ blog/ pesg -awareness -is -an -enduring -legacy -of -the -global -financial-crisisp-a5a9f2-en5/.
6. Niamh Moloney, *EU Securities and Financial Markets Regulation* (Oxford University Press 2023) 214.
7. Federal Ministry Republic of Austria: Climate Action, Environment, Energy, Mobility, Innovation and Technology, *European Sustainable Development Strategy* (2023) https:// www .bmk .gv .at/ en/ topics/ climate -environment/ sustainable-development/eu-sds.html.
8. Philippe Sands, *Principles of International Environmental Law* (Cambridge University Press 2003) 748.

9.   Nicola Notaro, 'International and European Environmental Law' in Paul Demaret, Inge Govaere, and Dominik Hanf, *European Legal Dynamics* (College of European Studies 2007) 527.

10. ibid 529.

11. European Commission, *Corporate Sustainability Reporting* (2023) https:// finance .ec .europa .eu/ capital -markets -union -and -financial -markets/ company -reporting -and -auditing/ company -reporting/ corporate -sustainability -reporting _en.

12. European Commission, *Action Plan: Financing Sustainable Growth* (2018) https:// eur -lex .europa .eu/ legal -content/ EN/ TXT/ PDF/ ?uri = CELEX: 52018DC0097.

13. Danny Busch, 'Sustainability Disclosure in the EU Financial Sector' in Danny Busch, Guido Ferrarini, and Seraina Grunewald, *Sustainable Finance in Europe: Corporate Governance, Financial Stability and Financial Markets* (Springer 2021) 397.

14. PRI, *Explaining the EU Action Plan for Financing Sustainable Growth* (2023) https:// www .unpri .org/ sustainable -financial -system/ explaining -the -eu -action -plan-for-financing-sustainable-growth/3000.article.

15. Danny Busch, 'EU Sustainable Finance Disclosure Regulation' (2023) Capital Markets Law Journal (Feb) 2.

16. Jos Delbeke, Elena Marro, and Peter Vis, *Towards an EU Policy Agenda for Voluntary Carbon Markets* (EUI 2023) https://cadmus.eui.eu/bitstream/handle/ 1814/75530/STG_PB_2023_08.pdf?sequence=4, 5.

17. Busch (n 15) 5.

18. European Commission, *Corporate Sustainability Reporting* (2023) https:// finance .ec .europa .eu/ capital -markets -union -and -financial -markets/ company -reporting -and -auditing/ company -reporting/ corporate -sustainability -reporting _en.

19. Grant Thornton, *Corporate Sustainability Reporting Directive (CSRD) – A Game-Changing EU Regulation* (2023) https:// www .grantthornton .global/ en/ insights/ articles/ corporate -sustainability -reporting -directive -csrd - - -a -game -changing-eu-regulation/.

20. Marius Fischer, *Disruptive and the Capital Markets: On Information, Risk and Uncertainty* (Walter de Gruyer 2023) 174.

21. Lucia Alessi and Georgios Papadopoulos, 'The EU regulatory Landscape on Sustainable Finance' in Pasquale Falcone and Edgardo Sica, *Sustainable Finance and the Global Health Crisis* (Routledge 2023) 134.

22. Aideen O'Dochartaigh, 'The Regulation Revolution: How Firms Can Prepare for ESG Disclosure Requirements' (2022) California Management Review 4.

23. Niamh Moloney, *EU Securities and Financial Markets Regulation* (Oxford University Press 2023) 214.

24. SEC, *Enhancement and Standardisation of Climate-Related Disclosures* (2022) https://www.sec.gov/files/33-11042-fact-sheet.pdf.

25. O'Dochartaigh (n 22) 3.

26. J.S. Nelson, 'The Future of Corporate Criminal Liability: Watching the ESG Space' (2022) SSRN. Available at https:// papers .ssrn .com/ sol3/ papers .cfm ?abstract_id=4057736 6.

27. David Hackett, Reagan Demas, Douglas Sanders, Jessica Wicha, and Aleesha Fowler, 'Growing ESG Risks: The Rise of Litigation' (2020) 50 Environmental Law Reporter 10849, 10850.

28. Rocio R Alamillos and Frederic de Mariz, 'How can European Regulation on ESG Impact Business Globally?' (2022) 15 Journal of Risk and Financial Management 291, 306.

29. Sierra Anderson, 'Criminalizing ESG: A Framework to Hold Corporations Accountable for Incorrect ESG Disclosures' (2023) 113 Journal of Criminal Law & Criminology 175, 180.

30. Connor Kuratek, Joseph A. Hall, and Betty M. Huber, 'Legal Liability for ESG Disclosures' (2020) Harvard Law School Forum on Corporate Governance (Aug 3) https:// corpgov .law .harvard .edu/ 2020/ 08/ 03/ legal -liability -for -esg -disclosures/#more-131560.

31. Emanuela Delbufalo, *Agency Theory and Sustainability in the Global Supply Chain* (Springer 2018) 1.

32. Gijs Jan Brandsma and Johan Adriaensen, 'The Principal-Agent Model, Accountability and Democratic Legitimacy' in Tom Delreux and Johan Adriaensen, *The Principal Agent Model and the European Union* (Springer 2017) 37.

33. Isaline Thirion, Patrick Reichert, Virginie Xhauflair, Jonathan De Jonck, 'From Fiduciary Duty to Impact Fidelity: Managerial Compensation in Impact Investing' (2022) 179 Journal of Business Ethics 4, 3.

34. Alessio Pacces, *Rethinking Corporate Governance: The Law and Economics of Control Powers* (Routledge 2013) 25.

35. ibid.

36. Michael C Jensen and William H Meckling, 'Theory of the Firm: Managerial Behaviour, Agency Costs and Ownership Structure' (1976) 3 Journal of Financial Economics 305–60, 308.

37. Delbufalo (n 31) 2.

38. Oliver Hart, 'An Economist's View of Fiduciary Duty' (1993) 43 The University of Toronto Law Journal 3 299–313, 300.

39. Thirion et al (n 33) 3.

40. Daniel Cash and Robert Goddard, *Investor Stewardship and the UK Stewardship Code: The Role of Institutional Investors in Corporate Governance* (Palgrave Macmillan 2021).

41. Freshfields Bruckhaus Deringer, *A Legal Framework for the integration of environmental social and governance issues into institutional investment* (2005) available at https://www.unepfi.org/fileadmin/documents/freshfields_legal_resp _20051123.pdf 6.

42. ClientEarth, *Our Groundbreaking Case Against Shell's Board of Directors* (2023) https://www.clientearth.org/latest/latest-updates/news/we-re-taking-legal -action-against-shell-s-board-for-mismanaging-climate-risk/.

43. Emmy Hawker, 'UK aims to end uncertainty on Fiduciary Duty' (2023) ESG Investor (Mar 30) https://www.esginvestor.net/uk-aims-to-end-uncertainty-on -fiduciary-duty/.

44. Jon McGowan, 'How a U.K. Case Could Impact Corporate Directors and ESG' (2023) Forbes (Mar 17) https://www.forbes.com/sites/jonmcgowan/2023/03/17/ how-a-uk-case-could-impact-corporate-directors-and-esg/.

45. Stephen Turner, 'Corporate Law, Directors' Duties and ESG Interventions: Analysing Pathways Towards Positive Corporate Impacts relating to ESG Issues' (2020) 4 Journal of Business Law 245–64, 254.

46. ibid 261.

47. Martin Lipton, 'Understanding the Role of ESG and Stakeholder Governance within the Framework of Fiduciary Duties' (2022) Harvard Law School Forum on Corporate Governance (Nov 29) https:// papers .ssrn .com/ sol3/ papers .cfm ?abstract_id=4294180 6.
48. ibid.
49. Pamela Hanrahan, 'Directors Duties and Public Interests' (2018) Presentation at the UNSW Centre for Law, Markets and Regulation Seminar Series (Apr 11) https://papers.ssrn.com/sol3/papers.cfm?abstract_id=3434936 8 (emphasis added).
50. Bruno Ferreira and Manuel Sequeira, 'Business Judgment Rule as a Safeguard for ESG minded Directors and a Warning for Others' in Paulo Camara and Filipe Morais, *The Palgrave Handbook of ESG and Corporate Governance* (Springer 2022) 275.
51. Roy Shapira, 'Mission Critical ESG and the Scope of Director Oversight Duties' (2022) SSRN. Available at https://papers.ssrn.com/sol3/papers.cfm?abstract_id= 4107748 9.
52. ibid 10.
53. ibid 12.
54. Todd Phillips, 'Director Engagement: Necessary for ESG Success' (2022) 52 Environmental Law Reporter 10641, 10643.
55. Leo E Strine, Kirby M Smith, and Reilly S Steel, 'Caremark and ESG, Perfect Together: A Practical Approach to Implementing an Integrated, Efficient, and Effective Caremark and EESG Strategy' (2021) 106 Iowa Law Review 1885, 1896.
56. Turner (n 45) 261.

4. The ESG rating sector

1. INTRODUCTION

The concept of an 'ESG rating agency' is a relatively new one. Even newer still is the concept of an agency providing simplified and correlated scores on the non-financial aspects of a company. However, analysis has shown that there is a distinct need for an independent third party to fill the asymmetric gap that exists in the post-Global Financial Crisis (GFC) world that seeks to examine businesses not only on their financial performance, but how they achieve it. There are also intrinsic questions that are being raised as we continue to witness the rise of the 'ESG rating agency' with regards to their focus, and how their analysis can feed into wider structures that already exist. In this chapter, we shall get to know the ESG rating sector better, inclusive of the challenges that the sector is currently facing.

At this point in the book, the scene has been set. The previous chapter alluded to wider legal and economic infrastructures that the ESG ratings may be able to assist. The wide usage of credit ratings, both for their informational value but also their ability to be used as signals, is clear. However, for the ESG ratings to find the same utility, some of the underlying facets in the credit rating space would need to be transplanted into the bourgeoning ESG rating space. It is, however, important to question whether this is the aim, because if we misunderstand that critical and foundational aspect to the industry, everything else that follows will be flawed.

There is also the issue of presumption. As we shall see in the first sector, the ESG rating space has its roots in providing assistance to investors who had very specific aims in terms of mobilising their investment in certain areas of society. The connotation of ESG is not universally agreed upon, meaning that the aims, objectives, and even the reason for ESG rating agencies existing is perhaps equally as contentious. If one believes that an ESG rating agency exists to understand the sustainability-related qualities of an entity, anything other than doing this will be seen as inefficient, less than useful, or, worse still, a betrayal of what has developed into a cultural movement. The stakes are high for ESG rating agencies, mainly because of the way the environment around them has developed in recent years.

As we shall discuss throughout the chapter, the ESG rating agencies were not responsible for the rise in what we shall call 'sustainable business'. Many – including me – have suggested that the 'movement' of pushing for business to be more sustainable is a direct reflection of the generational-defining wealth extraction that took place in the GFC. To my mind, we find similar system-altering approaches in history, with the 'New Deal' in the United States after the Wall Street Crash of 1929 and the ensuing Great Depression. Systemically, there has to be a 'response' of sorts in the aftermath of a systemic failure, if for nothing more than to be seen to provide a systemic antidote to what is clearly a systemic problem. The post-GFC sentiment has been focused on culture, mentality, and moving business-focused philosophies away from self and more towards the collective.

However, the rate of degeneration in business standards during the era of GFC in the 2000s meant that it was no longer enough just to say one will try to be better. The crucial element of *trust* had been reduced, which had immediate and lasting consequences. From that point on, business had to essentially show its workings, and demonstrably provide evidence that it was seeking to do better. As we saw in the last chapter, this was why the system responded with initiatives designed to increase disclosure rates, as well as improve the quality of disclosures. With initiatives focused on the duties of agents also being developed, the infrastructure around modern businesses was developed to provide layers of transparency and protection against another systemic collapse. Yet, there are critical elements to that infrastructure that the 'state', as an organ, cannot provide. Only the private sector can provide the perceived 'independence' needed to provide a system of signalling that market players can utilise to meet the necessary standards that are being put in place. In Chapter 2, where we focused on the credit rating agencies, we saw in detail how perhaps the most important (and I would argue genius) element of the whole credit rating sector is its overly simplistic signalling system. As we live in the economic era of the institutional investor, the dominance of the principal–agent relationship is tangible and it is against that backdrop that a simplistic signalling system of AAA being higher than C, for example, reveals its critical cleverness. To the disassociated principal investor, for example, the system is easier to understand with that rating scale applied. The actions of others, with one's resources, can be understood, constrained, regulated, and communicated quickly and simply. As the economy moves into the era of sustainability, the same disassociated aspect similarly affects all around it. Even though the economy is mostly controlled by 'universal owners'[1] – those large institutional investors that do not just own stakes in individual companies, but entire sectors – the principal–agent relationship still reigns supreme, even if there are increasingly more and more layers between the agent and the ultimate principal in the modern-day leviathans like BlackRock, Vanguard, and State Street. So, with that being understood, how likely is it that the principal that usually relies on credit ratings now understands the deluge of sustainability reports, shifting standards, and sustainability claims coming from companies their agents may be investing in? We can safely ask this same question when applied to the concept of their agents defining what they invest in (like within the European system of the taxonomy). Principals did not miraculously gain in-depth insight just because politicians have pushed for businesses to be sustainable.

It is within that familiar conundrum that we delve into understanding ESG rating agencies. The question that is new, however, is whether the ESG rating industry can meet those systemic needs. In the credit rating sector, the systemic configuration came afterwards, merely responding to the private organisational response to the underlying dilemma. Now, it is the other way around. The system is now actively being designed to meet identified needs, with the only reference point being the credit rating agencies that so spectacularly 'failed' only relatively recently. The challenge facing legislators, regulators, and politicians now is substantial, because getting it right is paramount, but getting it wrong could be catastrophic. I will go on to suggest that the only way in which the 'right' result can be achieved is to cede authority to the marketplace, and then reactively regulate and constrain, however uncomfortable one may find that notion (and I personally do). To understand why, we need to understand the ESG rating sector more.

2. THE PLAYERS

What the ESG rating agencies are designed to do is something that sits at the heart of the issues affecting the industry. The perception of their role, as opposed to how they actually operate, is actively leading to confusion, critical responses, and mis-regulation. Berg and his colleagues from the Aggregate Confusion Project provide us with a good place to start:

> ESG ratings first emerged in the 1980s as a service for investors to screen companies not purely on financial characteristics, but also on characteristics relating to social and environmental performance. The earliest ESG rating agency Vigeo-Eiris was established in 1983 in France and five years later Kinder, Lydenberg & Domini (KLD) was established in the US. While initially catering to a highly-specialized investor clientele, such as faith-based organisations, the market for ESG ratings has widened dramatically, especially in the past decade. Estimates are that 30 trillion USD are invested in ways that rely on some form of ESG information, a figure that has grown by 34 percent since 2016. As interest in sustainable investing grew, many early providers were acquired by established financial data providers, e.g. MSCI bought KLD in 2010, Morningstar bought Sustainalytics in 2010, ISS bought Oekom in 2018, and Moody's bought Vigeo-Eiris in 2019.[2]

This excerpt provides us with a variety of understandings. Not only has the growth in the industry been relatively recent, which has led to massive upheaval and movement within the industry itself, but the original objectives of the early ESG rating agencies are arguably no longer relevant. The highly specialised clientele that the scholars refer to in the quote tended to use ESG rating analysis to complement their already-substantial analytical toolkit, as they sought to filter or 'screen' investment opportunities to meet pre-existing (or developing) mandates. Those screens may include taking arms-related investments, or substance-related investments, out of their investment opportunity universe, for example. To do that, the investors would have utilised the skillsets of the early ESG rating agencies to decipher the underlying aspects of particular entities; these approaches were known as either 'ethical investing' or 'responsible investing' dependent upon how strict the investor was with their mandate.[3]

As time moved forward, the ESG rating agencies became more important. Some have attributed this to major political and organisational initiatives that have encouraged businesses to be more sustainable, like the UN Global Compact set forth in 2000,[4] but others have declared that it is both difficult to pinpoint a solitary reason for the industry's development, whilst also declaring that the total size and makeup of the ESG rating space is difficult to accurately measure.[5] That is likely for two reasons. The first is that there is a wide array of 'ESG rating agencies' varying greatly in size, from micro-entities to large international players. Second, very few entities are definitionally known as 'ESG rating agencies', mostly because, like most things relating to ESG and sustainability, there is no agreed-upon definition. Whilst the terminology of an 'ESG rating agency' is becoming more commonly accepted given that regulators are referring to them as ESG rating agencies, this was not always the case, with onlookers trying to capture the diversity in the field by referring to the entities as things like 'corporate sustainability systems' (CSSs), though this did not stick for long. As we shall see later in the chapter, not having an agreed-upon terminology to describe the business, or worse still, forcing one upon the industry itself, can and has led to real problems in the general understanding of what the industry exists to do, and what it is capable of. Third, large players like MSCI, Bloomberg, ISS, and the large credit rating agencies offer varying financial services simultaneously and not just ESG ratings, making it both difficult to classify them as 'ESG rating agencies', and they themselves unlikely to self-identify as 'ESG rating agencies'.

However, whilst a number of scholarly efforts have been undertaken to paint the picture of the ESG rating industry in all its glory,[6] one of the central initiatives is a report generated by the SustainAbility Institute by ERM, who develop their *Rate the Raters* report periodically. The report is really useful for us to get a broad understanding of the industry. For example, their most recent report starts by telling us:

> This year's Rate the Raters report is published at a tumultuous time for the ESG movement. ESG funds are growing rapidly, and the ESG performance of companies is being intensely scrutinized. Companies also face increasing ESG disclosure requirements, with regulators in Europe, the U.S., and other regions finalizing far-reaching new rules. At the same time, ESG is being painted as greenwashing by some of its detractors, and ESG raters face criticism over a lack of transparency and comparability in ESG data and rating methodologies.
>
> Within that context, our research highlights a paradox. Thanks to the growing emphasis on ESG performance, ratings are more widely used than ever. At the same time, investors and companies show only moderate confidence in the accuracy and utility of ESG ratings. These trends cannot comfortably co-exist, suggesting that significant changes will be needed in order to maintain the future credibility of the ratings ecosystem.[7]

The report provides us with a helpful infographic that presents 13 top players in the field (see Table 4.1 for the derivation). The table is revealing. It shows an Anglo-American-dominated industry that contains some of the world's largest financial service players, like Bloomberg, the London Stock Exchange, MSCI, and of course the three big credit rating agencies. It also shows the space for specialist agencies like CDP and EcoVadis, though one could argue this is the same in the credit rating space with players such as AM Best and Demotech.

It is also revealing that the majority of ESG rating agencies focus their attention on serving institutional investors, which makes sense when we see the vocal critique coming from institutional investors whenever they are surveyed for their opinions on the efficacy of the ESG rating space. Again, there is some space for specialists who focus on supply chains (CDP and EcoVadis) or providing information for due diligence procedures (RepRisk). But for the most part, the core customer is the institutional investor, which provides us with an anchor to understand (a) when we ask about how useful an ESG rating agency is, by whose definition are we relating to, and (b) what do the core customers of the ESG rating agencies actually want? By understanding who they are, these questions can be answered (which we will do later).

Other key elements of the table come in the inter-relationships between the 'Access to Methodology', 'Coverage of ESG', and 'Source of Information for Primary ESG Rating' columns because, arguably, they are all intertwined. Being able to view the methodological considerations of an agency is tremendously useful, especially when compared with the way they consider ESG information generally, and then critically how they are sourcing that information. For example, by using those columns we can see that ISS-ESG, as just one random example, does not make the methodologies public, only generally covers ESG information, and takes a passive approach to sourcing

ESG information (usually by way of scanning publicly available documents, for example). In opposition to this approach, S&P's ESG arm has their methodology fully public, does cover ESG information generally, but actively sources information from entities (although this approach changed in 2023 to one of asking surveyed issuers to input publicly available data). Interestingly, the Big Three rating agencies all differ in their approaches to making the methodologies public, covering ESG information, and sourcing information. Also, only one ESG rating agency can boast having their methodologies fully public, covering ESG information in a specialised manner, and actively sourcing their information for their ratings: CDP. One may muse whether this is because they are a non-profit charity, with the only other charity on the list (JUST Capital) only differing in the fact that they do not actively source the underlying data for their ratings, but instead use publicly available data.

If you are wondering about what is meant by active or passive data generation, the difference describes whether the ESG rating agency actively engages with the target company, or simply utilises whatever publicly available data there is. Jumping forward into the next section for a moment, there are distinct problems with these approaches. For those that actively engage with companies to retrieve data, there is no set way with which to do this, and all of the ESG rating agencies that take this approach do so *at the same time*. The duplication costs are obvious, and it is no wonder that surveyed issuers find this to be a real issue, with the report finding that 'most corporations are usually rated by ten or more ESG raters'. For passive raters, the problem lies not in duplicative costs for issuers, but in either misunderstanding or simply misrepresenting the data one finds. In the report, issuers are clear that there are major issues with the interpretation of public information ESG rating agencies find, with some remarking that they have to strenuously comb through the ESG ratings on their company to make sure the underlying data is correct, which it often is not:

> ...the data captured from our company is often incorrect, and we have to comb through ratings reports to find and fix errors. In one analysis of an ESG data provider, we found that over 50 percent of the information required adjustments.

It is therefore not surprising that other issuers have suggested that 'given the limitations of most rater and ranker methodologies today, only those that require meticulous engagement via a questionnaire are rated Very High quality'.[8] This is just one small but representative example of the concept of divergence in the sector and its effects.

Additionally, the above is also a representation of the mixed signals in the ESG rating space. One is often told that there are too many requests of issuers, leading to duplication costs but, at the same time, one is also told that those

Table 4.1 Comparison table of ESG ratings providers

	Main Customer Base	Ownership	Headquarters Location	Access to Methodology	Coverage of ESG	Source of Information for Primary ESG Rating
Bloomberg	Institutional investors	Private company	USA	Accessible via Bloomberg Terminal	Generalised	Passive
CDP	Institutional investors, Supply chain partners	Non-profit charity	UK	Public in full	Specialised	Active
EcoVadis	Supply chain partners	Private (pre-IPO startup)	France	Overview only	Specialised	Active
FTSE4Good	Institutional investors	London Stock Exchange subsidiary	UK	Overview only	Generalised	Passive
ISS-ESG	Institutional investors	Deutsche Börse subsidiary	USA	Not public	Generalised	Passive
Just Capital	Stakeholders and the public	Non-profit charity	USA	Public in full	Specialised	Passive
Moody's ESG	Institutional investors	Public company	USA	Not public	Generalised	Passive
MSCI	Institutional investors	Public company	USA	Public in full	Generalised	Passive
Refinitiv	Institutional investors	London Stock Exchange subsidiary	UK	Public in full	Generalised	Passive
RepRisk	Other ESG raters, Third-party due diligence for M&A	Private company	Switzerland	Public in full	Specialised	Passive
S&P Global ESG	Institutional investors	Public company	Switzerland	Public in full	Generalised	Active

	Main Customer Base	Ownership	Headquarters Location	Access to Methodology	Coverage of ESG	Source of Information for Primary ESG Rating
Sustainable Fitch	Institutional investors	Hearst subsidiary	USA	Overview only	Generalised	Passive
Sustainalytics	Institutional investors	Morningstar subsidiary	Netherlands	Overview only	Generalised	Passive

Source: The SustainAbility Institute by ERM, *Rate the Raters 2023: ESG Ratings at a Crossroads* (2023), 11, https://www.sustainability.com/globalassets/sustainability.com/thinking/pdfs/2023/rate-the-raters-report-april-2023.pdf.

that seek information directly from issuers are more trusted, and it is those ESG rating agencies who take such a direct approach that have more accurate and reliable ratings as opposed to those with passive approaches. This is confusing, and even more so when we understand that perhaps the most thorough and well-respected ESG rating entity, S&P's newly acquired Corporate Sustainability Assessment (CSA), changed its methodology to one of providing links to public disclosures, rather than issuers submitting direct answers and responses to the CSA.[9] The CSA – which was part of RobecoSAM before S&P purchased the SAM CSA from RobecoSAM in 2019 – has been widely regarded as one of the leading mechanisms for understanding an issuer's true position, arguably alongside the work of CDP. However, in 2023 S&P announced that it wanted to 'streamline data requirements and reduce the length of the questionnaire', whilst also altering the components of the questionnaire to focus on key aspects, as S&P see them.[10]

With industry-leading initiatives scaling back what they are asking of issuers, it is probably wise to consider the models that ESG rating agencies use and, also, who pays for them. Interestingly, as the EU found during their investigations into the lead-up to their recent 2023 ESG Ratings Regulatory Proposal (which we shall review at the end of this chapter):

> the 'investor pays' model appears to be commonly used. Investors pay a fee depending on the type and range of products they wish to access, as well as the level of granularity and method of access to data: 'headline' ESG ratings or underlying information, current or historical ratings, delivery channel, etc.[11]

We will assess where the ESG rating space may be in its ultimate arc, but it is noted that the credit rating agencies too began by charging investors, until their environment changed and allowed for issuers to be leveraged.

However, this pay model is not universal. Whilst the 'investor pays' model has its critics – like those who argue that the model does not really allow for great exposure to issuers – only a handful of ESG rating agencies adopt the 'issuer pays' model like the dominant credit rating agencies do, with an example being Standard Ethics. Yet, in the ESG rating space, this has only taken the form of being solicited by an issuer to conduct a rating based on publicly available data, not sensitive data as of yet.[12] Irrespective of the pay model, all ESG rating agencies will conduct their approach in one of two ways: either with questionnaire-driven methods, or analyst-driven methods. To explain, Landi et al. discuss how questionnaires are usually utilised by those using the investor-pays model, as it allows them to 'update a database and provide tailor-made analysis to various institutional investors', whilst those utilising analyst-driven ratings operate like the credit rating agencies, where an analyst or team of analysts will lead on developing the rating for an entity. As described by Landi et al.:

> Typically, analysts obtain information from published and publishable reports, as well as from interviews and discussions with the applicant's management. They use that information and apply their analytical judgement to assess the entity's sustainability condition, operating performance, policies, and risk management strategies and reputational risk. This approach is similar to the one adopted by credit rating agencies. Standard Ethics, acting as a solicited sustainability rating (SSR) agency, adopts this model.[13]

With one of the leading questionnaires in the marketplace being 'streamlined' by S&P, there is room to question whether that approach will be maintained despite its popularity. The *Rate the Raters* report, which surveyed a variety of 'users' of ESG ratings, found clear support for the approach, with CDP and S&P ESG scoring near the top consistently when survey respondents were asked to rank the 'usefulness' of particular ESG rating agencies (and also for perceived 'quality', coincidentally).

Before we move on, it is a good idea to pause for a moment and ask the question, 'what does usefulness mean with regards to ESG ratings?' The respondents to the *Rate the Raters* report suggested that they mainly use ESG ratings to (a) supplement their organisation's own research on ESG issues, and almost at the same rate because (b) there is a growing demand by key stakeholders, including clients, to use the ESG ratings provided by ESG rating agencies. What is of interest to us – though it is not answered in the report itself – is *why* key stakeholders want investment managers to use ESG ratings (it is no surprise at this point that, for this book at least, the argument is that it is because of the need to signal).

One can see quite clearly, even from the perspective of understanding how ESG rating agencies approach the business of generated ESG ratings, that there are major issues. These issues are widespread and are quickly becoming synonymous with the concept of ESG ratings more broadly, allowing the sector to be caught up in the so-called 'culture wars' that are blighting western democracies. The inefficiencies, which we shall cover next, are often held out as representations and examples of why ESG does not work, or at least should not be championed. We shall see now whether these issues are inherent to the concept of ESG rating, or emblematic of the early stages of a critical sector that needs to evolve.

3.   THE ISSUES

There are a variety of issues that are currently affecting the ESG rating space. The culmination of these issues has led to wide-ranging regulatory efforts currently being designed around the world. However, some of the issues are more technical in nature, whilst others are more philosophical, meaning that resolving the 'issues' affecting the ESG rating space is very difficult indeed. In this section we shall assess these issues, which will give us the foundation with which to understand the regulatory efforts that are being developed. However, before we do that, there are some key questions to answer.

The first is the role, or even the authority, of the regulator in this equation. We saw in the earlier parts of the book that the regulators in the credit rating space have always been primarily reactive in nature, responding to market practices and aiming to inject official authority for the protection of vulnerable groups, like consumers. However, in the ESG rating space, the ascendency is so recent that the task being faced by regulators and legislators is very different. Whilst we shall ask the question of how best to approach the task of instilling order in the ESG rating space in the next section, here we need to ask how that mandate affects one's understandings of the issues being faced by the ESG rating space. For instance, one of the most tangible concerns for legislators and regulators is that they do not want to 'bake in' bad practices by accident and be left with both the need to fix the processes and being culpable for consolidating them. The risk of unintended regulator consequences is extraordinarily high at this point in the ESG rating sector's development.

However, there are issues that arise, like the early signs of oligopolistic behaviour via mergers and acquisitions, that a legislator/regulator dare not touch. Enforcing competition in the credit rating space has been an unmitigated disaster, so it is likely that the same mistake will not be actively repeated. Yet, another major issue is the lack of clarity surrounding the entire concept of ESG. With such a changing definitional landscape, effectively regulating those supposedly designed to rate against the concept brings with it inherent difficulties. Perhaps one of the biggest issues, however is understanding what an ESG rating agency exists to do.

If one were to ask what a credit rating agency technically exists to do, the answer is straightforward. A credit rating agency exists to determine the likelihood that an investor will be paid back, and whether that will be in full and on time. The credit rating agency has morphed into an entirely different beast beyond that simple definition, of course, but at its core it simply exists to assess the creditworthiness of an entity. However, in the ESG rating space, it could not be more complicated. This is because, philosophically, the concept of ESG has no particular 'home'. Initially conceptualised to be a simple categorisation of issues that issuers and especially investors could gauge against, in order to conduct business more sustainably, the concept of ESG has evolved into something different. Arguably, it has become whatever one wants it to be, which is relatively dangerous. It is dangerous because of its adaptability in modern-day parlance, which it was never intended to be. For instance, it does not mean screened investing, and nor does it mean social surveillance. In that realm of it being all things to all people, the role of an ESG rating agency has similarly caused consternation.

Recent media articles have focused on this perceived inequity between seemingly environmentally friendly companies, and those that may have traditionally been categorised as 'sin stocks'. One article references the fact that Tesla scored 37 out of 100, whilst Philip Morris International (the owner of the brand 'Marlboro') scored 84 out of 100. It also discusses the recent outburst by Elon Musk because of the fact that ExxonMobil was rated in the top 10 of S&P 500's ESG index, whilst Tesla was excluded entirely, to which Musk remarked the whole process was a 'scam' that 'has been weaponised by phony social justice warriors'.[14] Rather than analysing Musk's contribution to the so-called 'culture wars', instead it would be better to ask just how an ESG rating agency could give a so-called 'sin stock' such a high rating, whilst one of the most prominent electric vehicle manufacturers could be so widely and poorly regarded?

The answer, as it often does, lies in perception. Musk is making the mistake of assuming that an ESG rating agency is concerned with the 'ESGness' of an entity, for want of a better word. He presumes that if a company is contributing positively to society, as he believes his company does, then it should be rewarded with a high ESG score. However, in reality, ESG rating agencies are not concerned with that aspect in the slightest. Rather, they are concerned with what is often called a 'single materiality' approach, as opposed to the 'double materiality' approach that Musk is suggesting. Technically, single materiality in this context is described as 'the impact of society and the natural world on an entity's financial performance', whereas double materiality is described as 'the impact of the firm on society and the natural world'.[15] As Mayer helpfully and simply contextualises for us, 'so, for example, climate change might affect the performance of a firm – single materiality – or the firm might contribute to climate change – double materiality'. Perhaps the easiest way is to think of it directionally – one is inward-facing from the perspective of the company, and one is outward-facing. Musk and many (and I mean the majority of onlookers) who are not specially concerned with this field presume that an ESG rating agency exists to understand ESG concerns from a double-materiality standpoint because, to them (and one can understand why), it is logical for that to be the case.

However, in 2022, the chairman and CEO of MSCI took to the professional social media platform LinkedIn to pen an article entitled *ESG Ratings: Setting the Record Straight*, within which he addressed this issue directly. Henry Fernandez starts bluntly, declaring directly:

> MSCI's ESG ratings are not a report card on corporate citizenship. Instead, they are investment tools that measure a company's resilience to long-term, financially material environmental, social, and governance risks.[16]

There are two key elements in this excerpt. The first relates to the measurement of a company's *resilience*, which is perhaps the critical element to understand if one wants to understand how Philip Morris International can outscore Tesla so greatly. Whilst not seeking to compare the two ratings (because as we shall discuss shortly, that is extremely problematic), the fact that Philip Morris International invests so heavily in its legal defence, and also diversifies so greatly in its product range are all positive attributes for the ESG rating analysts, irrespective of whether it is a sin stock. Critics argue that this means one can do societal harm, as long as they invest in the legal defence to reduce the consequences for the company's bottom line, which in effect is a strong argument. This is a strong argument mainly because of the second critical element of the excerpt above, which is that the ESG rating measures a company's resilience against long-term *financially material* ESG risks. The risks need to be potentially and prospectively attributable to the company's financial position for the ESG analyst to be concerned, which is the definition of single materiality.

Fernandez, for his part, blames journalists for the confusion: 'the confusion begins when journalists imply that "sustainable investing", "climate investing", and "ESG investing" are synonymous. That is incorrect. In fact, those terms cover a broad range of ESG approaches.' He goes on to say some investors will look to improve social or environmental outcomes through their investments, which he labels 'impact investing', whilst others may seek to align their investments with their ethical or moral stance, which he labels 'values-based investing'. He is correct in his definitions, but his mistake is revealed in his arrogance of deciding to define what ESG investing is, and what it is not. Nobody has ever declared that impact investing and values-based investing are under the umbrella of 'ESG investing'. In fact, it is quite the opposite, with those branches often being separated, and for good reason. This relates to another matter which is important, though a slight deviation for us. The arrogance of defining what something is for the planet, without consultation, is a flaw without equal. Alex Michalos discusses this phenomenon in relation to the early works of what is today Sustainalytics, who, through their early products, sought to both define and then rank what different types of investing were, and under what umbrella. In relation to the earlier concept of corporate social responsibility (CSR), somewhat of a precursor to the concept of ESG (potentially):

> These comments suggest that different people have different ideas about exactly what should be counted as CSR activities and the value of praising or blaming companies for their performance of such activities. There is not a great deal of agreement on the meaning of basic concepts connected to CSR, on appropriate assessment criteria, data availability, measurement, aggregation, and auditing procedures. In short, the field is ripe of exploitation, and no one should be surprised in companies like *Maclean's* and Jantzi-Sustainalytics find a profitable niche in the field.[17]

Michalos here is discussing the conjoined report on the *Top 50 Socially Responsible Corporations* between Maclean and Jantzi-Sustainalytics, as it was then known, but the concept is clear to understand. With the inability to definitively define the concept of ESG being abundantly clear, the arrogance of doing so as a for-profit company can quickly escalate into exploitation, as Michalos would call it, and it is difficult to see past this understanding.

Fernandez concludes what amounts to a sales pitch by declaring: 'ESG ratings are not a *replacement* for climate-focused investment tools, they are a *complement* to climate-focused investment tools... MSCI is proud to offer both.' This is yet another demonstration of his determination to define the field, but as was mentioned earlier, defining what ESG ratings are and what they are not, in a diverse field, is not a wise decision. Irrespective of this, the definitional issues are not resolved by Fernandez's declarations, but it does position their predominantly single-materiality-based approach nicely – though it is important to make clear that not all ESG rating agencies, as we know them, are so clearly out to focus on the health and wellbeing of the corporation. Others, like CDP, for example, are distinctly clear that their approach is based on double materiality.[18]

Yet, definitions are the tip of the iceberg. The full iceberg is made up of technical issues that continue to plague the nascent industry. Criticism has been forthcoming for the ESG rating agencies since, well, the start of the industry.[19] Early research that surveyed the industry's users (precursors to the *Rate the Raters* report that has since become a staple) revealed a variety of issues for the early stages of the industry, which were to be expected, like the majority of the 700 respondents being entirely unfamiliar with many ESG rating agencies and their products and indices. Additionally, 'survey fatigue' was identified early as being a key issue for those that did engage with the early ESG rating agencies.[20]

Escrig-Olmedo et al. note that the growth in the early ESG rating space, especially as more generalised entities came to the fore, resulted in issues for the industry that have continued throughout. Of the key challenges, scholars suggest that the following are the key concerns:

1. Lack of transparency. ESG rating agencies do not offer complete and public information about the criteria and the assessment process developed by them to evaluate the corporate sustainability performance. This makes understanding what ESG rating agencies are measuring and making comparisons between them difficult.
2. Commensurability. ESG rating agencies may measure the same concept in different ways. Therefore, if the assessments of ESG ratings are not consistent, which involves evidence of low commensurability, the hypothesised benefits of CSR cannot occur.
3. Trade-offs among criteria. ESG ratings methodologies may compensate higher scores in one domain with very low scores in another domain.
4. Lack of an overall score. Most of the ESG rating agencies provide environmental, social and governance ratings to each domain, but they do not provide an overall score of the corporate sustainability performance.
5. Stakeholders' preferences. ESG rating agencies do not address the different stakeholders' expectations in their evaluation processes, which influences their acceptance and usefulness.[21]

This evaluation is useful and provides for a solid starting point for us to consider the issues affecting the ESG rating space.

One of the more headline-grabbing issues, apart from the focus on materiality (single or double), is what is known as commensurability. In the context of ESG ratings, this means 'having a common measure', especially amongst and between the ratings of the various agencies. It stands to reason that the more ESG rating agencies that exist, the likelihood of having high levels of commensurability decreases, but research has honed in on this issue and revealed critical failings, which the ESG rating space, as yet, has no answer for. Escrig-Olmedo et al. find:

> [There is] strong evidence of low commensurability of SRI ratings; that is, raters continue to have low agreement even when we adjust for explicit differences in what they say they are trying to measure. When commensurability is low, then all or most raters have high measurement error when trying to measure similar theoretical constructs. These results call into question the validity of social ratings, which impact managerial actions around the world, guide trillions of dollars of investment, and inform scholarly perspectives on corporate social responsibility.[22]

Berg et al. – in representing the MIT-based Aggregate Confusion Project, which focuses specifically on this issue – agree, and reveal that 53% of the discrepancies they find in relation to the accuracy of ESG ratings 'comes from the fact that the rating agencies are measuring the same categories differently'.[23] Of interest here is what the ESG rating agencies are actually disagreeing on, with research revealing surprising results. For instance, Berg et al. note that there is evidence of acceptable agreement on aspects such as environmental policy (0.57) but, on things which the agencies can factually check, there is low agreement between the agencies. As explained by the scholars:

> However, most categories exhibit lower correlations. Surprisingly, even categories that measure straightforward facts that are easily obtained from public records have very heterogeneous levels of correlation. Membership in the UN Global Compact and CEO/Chairman separation, for instance, show correlations of 0.86 and 0.56, respectively. There are also a number of negative correlations. They appear mostly in categories of the social dimension, such as responsible marketing and occupational health and safety, but also in the category toxic spills. This indicates that the level of disagreement is so severe on some categories that rating agencies reach not just different, but even opposite conclusions.[24]

The subjectivity that is inherent within the non-financial realm means that disagreement between agencies will likely be common, and one could argue accepted. Many have declared (though I personally question such declarations) that variance and diversity of opinion is welcomed in the space. But, disagreements on whether an entity is signed up to an international framework, as just one example, is not acceptable; the entity either is or is not signed up, and the agencies should be fact-checking this before including the data in the rating. Such 'divergence' is proving difficult to ignore, and the industry's critics are honing in on such instances as validation for their wider-ranging criticisms. It has been suggested that instances such as these are a representation of the opacity in the ESG rating space, which conceals a cycle of poor informational processes; the inability to 'see under the hood', as is said in the US, means errors that are revealed are in a sense magnified and extrapolated, instead of there being clear rationales for differences, i.e., unable to obtain certain information, not having the right technology to integrate the data, or whatever else the issue may be, short of simply not checking the data (which would be unforgivable for a for-profit rating agency).[25]

Berg et al. followed up their research on the divergence between ESG rating agencies with an interesting conclusion that focused on what they called 'the rater effect'. They described this as 'a firm that is perceived as good will be seen through a positive lens and receive better indicator scores than the individual indicator would have allowed for, and vice versa'. In seeking explanations to this phenomenon, the scholars found that some agencies make it impossible for entities to get higher scores if they do not fill in the questionnaires properly:

> While speaking to RobecoSAM we learned about another potential cause for such a rater effect. Some raters make it impossible for firms to receive a good indicator score if they do not give an answer to the corresponding question in the questionnaire. This happens regardless of the actual indicator performance. The extent to which the firms answer specific questions is very likely correlated across indicators. Hence, the willingness to disclose might also explain parts of the rater effect.[26]

This obviously brings into question the processes within the ESG rating agencies. An associated question becomes, then, whether a high score is reflective of the underlying quality of the entity in a particular category or perspective, or whether they are good at meeting the procedural needs of the ESG rating agencies. The obvious effect of this latter question was discussed by the OECD:

> Methodological concerns also arise when looking at the final ESG product. External research and OECD analysis indicates an implicit ESG scoring bias in favour of large-cap companies and against SMEs. This is reflected in the OECD analysis of ESG ratings compared to market capitalisation and may be due to the fact that SMEs do not have the resources to invest in non-financial disclosure, as the costs may outweigh the investment gains in the near term. However, this bias, and the hurdle of unlocking useful ESG information from smaller companies, creates a market inefficiency that affects both the relative cost of capital and corporate reputation.
>
> There is some evidence that this bias also exists with respect to ESG scores among Emerging Market Issuers. As there is lower ESG disclosure practice in parts of EMEs, some companies with sound practices with respect to environment, social and governance issues could be penalised because they do not yet disclose their assessment of ESG risks and opportunities in a manner consistent with emerging good practice.[27]

This is extremely problematic. It is problematic because different jurisdictions have very different compositions in terms of how they do business. An example is that whilst the US is heavily corporatised, places like the EU have a large amount of SMEs. With a large majority of ESG rating agencies being housed in the US, especially the largest and arguably most influential, there is a real risk of American hegemony being fundamentally integrated into the global financial architecture by way of new non-financial-based ratings from the ESG rating agencies.

It is not difficult to see why the challenge facing regulators is a complex one. However, that complex challenge exists in a dualised fashion, because the environment can affect the trajectory of the ESG ratings. Research has focused on how the ESG rating agencies considered various indicators and then assessed this against the backdrop of major political movements, like the Paris Climate Accord in 2015, after which research revealed that ESG rating agencies fundamentally increased their focus on the climate-related outputs of companies in the aftermath of the 2015 accord.[28] The point here to connect to the issue of the rater effect is that the emergence of regulatory scrutiny from places like the EU, who will seek to protect their constituents (the majority of whom are SMEs), means that things may have to change in the underlying approach of the ESG rating agencies if they are to adapt to the changing environment around them.

Other relevant issues include the informational flow that has been discussed throughout this book. As we saw in Chapter 2, their common claim is that they are a slave to the information they are given, and do not exist to be auditors of the information they receive (the sentiment being that an industry already exists to meet this critical societal function). This concept of auditing and its interconnection to the concept of ESG is of paramount importance because, as Del Giudice and Rigamonti suggest, 'rating agencies provide accurate measures of companies' sustainability when the underlying non-financial information is audited'.[29] However, as Garcia et al. discuss, many aspects of the indicators that ESG rating agencies will rely upon cannot confidently be measured and therefore not audited.[30] Yet, the new CSRD in the EU mandates that underlying sustainability claims made by companies must be audited, which has the potential to either improve the informational flow that the ESG rating agencies will take advantage of (theoretically), or produce audit certificates for things which cannot be audited, leading to an injection of 'greenwashing' into the financial sector. Consequently, the growth of the ESG assurance sector, dominated by the traditional auditing entities, is significant.[31]

The issues affecting the ESG rating space are complex and highly variable. They also transition through different times and spaces, and affect different ESG rating entities differently. On top of this, there are also regional differences as to how these issues manifest themselves, whilst there are also varied differences in how the ESG rating actually affects different components of different regions. The key word in that sentence, unsurprisingly, was 'differences'. Unfortunately, that word is inherently attributed to the nascent sector and is a word which is not necessarily positive in the field of ratings. The reason why is something we shall address in the next two chapters, but the effects are clear to see. An array of identified issues, supported by consistent and quite damaging criticism, means the ESG rating space is not progressing easily. Critics have made the point that 'it is ironic that the rating and ranking agencies that complain of the lack of transparency in corporate reporting often lack transparency themselves', but this is tempered by the admission that 'it is also due to the failure of regulatory authorities to set adequate standards for alignment of data and reporting requirements'.[32] The reality is that the ESG rating agencies are a function within a system and, whilst they may not be operating as efficiently as the system would like, the problem is a systemic one, not an industrial one. The right infrastructure must be designed for the ESG rating agencies to properly play the role the system needs them to. With that in mind, we need to consider the regulatory response to this array of issues.

4.   THE REGULATORY RESPONSE

Financial regulation, like most other forms of regulation, follows a particular pattern. In relation to ratings, a regulatory body usually has to be incentivised to allocate scarce resources into regulating a particular industry, especially from the ground up. This process is revealed when assessing how the move to regulate ESG rating agencies has taken shape across the globe. With different jurisdictions meeting the challenge in a variety of ways, the reasoning for that difference can be found in cultural aspects, or in relation to the dynamics of their domestic markets.

The growing body of academic research, the likes of which have been referenced throughout this book, started to turn attention towards the ESG rating space, its growing importance, the views of key stakeholders, and ultimately provided critical insight into the issues affecting the progression of the industry. Also, crucially, that critical insight positioned the ESG rating space within the wider economic picture and revealed the needs that key stakeholders like investors had. What was a common theme was that action needed to be taken to resolve some of the prohibitive issues affecting the utility of the ESG rating space, with some pushing for full regulation and others pushing for guided parameters to be erected.

However, for domestic or even continental legislators/regulators like the European Commission to take action requires a starting point which academia alone cannot provide. To start the wheels turning within such massive infrastructures like the EU, it is often the role of IOSCO that can get the regulatory machinery started. So, with that in mind, we will start our review of regulatory developments in the ESG rating space with the proposed guidance from IOSCO, which set the global wheels in motion, and then review key jurisdictions and where they are in their quest to inject authority into the nascent ESG rating space.

4.1   IOSCO

On 21 November 2021, the International Organization of Securities Commissions (IOSCO) produced its 'Final Report' on ESG ratings and data products providers after consultation.[33] The body, made up of securities regulators from around the world, had set out on a fact-finding mission to respond to the growing focus on ESG ratings and data providers, and provide regulatory guidance, if needed, so that jurisdictions with an interest in ESG ratings may move forward if appropriate. IOSCO started its consultative process based upon the following findings, which it found to be integral to the ESG rating space:

- There is little clarity and alignment on definitions, including on what ratings or data products intend to measure.
- There is a lack of transparency about the methodologies underpinning these ratings or data products.
- While there is wide divergence within the ESG ratings and data products industry, there is an uneven coverage of products offered, with certain industries or geographical areas benefitting from more coverage than others, thereby leading to gaps for investors seeking to follow certain investment strategies.
- There may be concerns about the management of conflicts of interest where the ESG ratings and data products provider or an entity closely associated with the provider performs consulting services for companies that are the subject of these ESG ratings or data products.
- Better communication with companies that are the subject of ESG ratings or data products was identified as an area meriting further attention given the importance of ensuring the ESG ratings or other data products are based on sound information.

In response to their initial consultation based upon the findings above, IOSCO received a total of 61 responses, which were mostly supportive of the endeavour shown by IOSCO and mostly agreed with the initial proposals set out in the consultative document.

The Final Report starts by understanding the market, and they introduce a very helpful table that shows the sheer scale of the merger and acquisition activity in the space over the short period of just four years (Table 4.2).[34] It only runs up to 2020 and does not include major acquisitions, like S&P's acquisition of IHS Markit for more than $40 billion, but it is still very useful to show the scale of activity. It is confirmed that there is an array of smaller providers who offer distinct specialisms for very particular areas of the market, but that these smaller providers are susceptible to being devoured by the largest players, who have, for the most part, retained the legal status of the smaller players after acquisition via subsidiarisation. The report then goes on to make the necessary definitional determinations between ESG rating providers and ESG data providers, and offers examples and illustrations for the businesses of the two industries.

The report then moves onto the issue of regulation, confirming the state of play in 2021 that no ESG rating regulations had been established anywhere

Table 4.2   *Examples of recent mergers and acquisitions in the ESG*
               ratings and data provision market

Year	Target	Acquirer
2016	Trucost (UK)	S&P Global (US)
2017	Sustainalytics (Netherlands) – acquisition of a 40% stake	Morningstar (US)
	South Pole (Switzerland) (Investment Climate Data Division)	ISS (US)
2018	Solaron (India)	Sustainalytics (Netherlands)
	Oekom (Germany)	ISS (US) (acquired in 2020 by Deutsche Börse Group)
2019	Video-Eiris (France)	Moody's Corp (US)
	Beyond Ratings (France)	London Stock Exchange (UK)
	Four Twenty Seven (US)	Moody's Corp (US)
	GES International (Sweden)	Sustainalytics (Netherlands)
	Carbon Delta (Switzerland)	MSCI (US)
	SynTao Green Finance (China) – minority stake	Moody's Corp (US)
	Ethical Corp (US)	Thomson Reuters (US)
	RobecoSAM AG-ESG ratings business (Switzerland)	S&P Global (US)
2020	Sustainalytics (Netherlands) – 100% stake	Morningstar (US)
	EcoVadis (France) – Non-controlling interest	CVC Growth Partners (US)
	TrueValueLab (US)	Factset (US)

Source: IOSCO, *Environmental, Social and Governance (ESG) Ratings and Data Products Providers: Final Report* (2021) https://www.iosco.org/library/pubdocs/pdf/IOSCOPD690.pdf.

in the world, with only voluntary codes of conduct being established. IOSCO confirmed this understanding:

> IOSCO considered the existence of regulatory requirements or voluntary standards in members' jurisdictions. These could provide a real-world example of regulatory or standard setting requirements for these activities or indicate where there may be potential for overlap or conflict with any of IOSCO's proposed recommendations. IOSCO took a bottom-up approach to this scoping exercise, asking the ESG ratings and data products providers whether they were subject to any supervisory or regulatory frameworks. The feedback received identified only a limited number of national regulatory frameworks applicable to providers of these or similar products. For example, the legal and regulatory framework in the EU for benchmarks and

United Kingdom may be relevant for certain providers of benchmarks with an ESG or climate dimension.

However, this framework is not directly relevant for the broad scope of ESG ratings and data products as described and foreseen in this report. As a result, the current situation would appear to be one in which there are few examples of legal and regulatory frameworks of direct relevance for ESG ratings and data products, and no voluntary frameworks of direct relevance, outside of those being applied more generally by providers of Financial Benchmarks.

The report noted that a handful of jurisdictions had initiated very early-stage investigations into the role of ESG rating agencies, mostly in relation to wider remits like the EU's 'Action Plan' in 2018 or the UK's focus on ESG issues in the capital markets in 2021. It was on this almost blank canvas that IOSCO presented its recommendations.

The first recommendation IOSCO put forward was that *regulators could consider focusing more attention on the use of ESG ratings and data products, and ESG ratings and data products providers that may be subject to their jurisdiction.* This was the starter's pistol that would bring about the race to regulate ESG rating agencies across the world. Within this recommendation IOSCO suggested that regulators should assess whether ESG rating agencies were covered by existing frameworks or whether there was any 'overlap' that may be present that could either reduce regulatory costs or lead to duplicative efforts if not identified. Also, the report suggests that regulators could decide to support voluntary efforts to develop base standards. In terms of what base standards should be pursued, the report suggests that conflicts of interests and mitigative procedures should be declared, along with pursuing transparency across issues of internal governance structures, methodologies and their transmission, and aspects such as analyst training and avenues for complaints.

The second recommendation was for ESG rating agencies and data providers, suggesting that *ESG ratings and data providers could consider adopting and implementing written procedures designed to help ensure the issuance of high-quality ESG ratings and data products based on publicly disclosed data sources where possible and other information sources where necessary, using transparent and defined methodologies.* One may be thinking that any ESG rating agency seeking to stay profitable (or in the case of non-profits, seeking to stay alive and relevant) would be doing all of the above anyway, but the key with this recommendation is that it all can be translated and transmitted in a way which others can objectively observe and understand. The concepts of methodologies being publicly scrutinised may seem normal in the credit rating space, but we must remember that this only started in the aftermath of the GFC. Having transparent processes connected to the concept of 'rating' in the financial sector is certainly relatively new, and very much abnormal for ratings providers. This recommendation sets the scene for that approach to transparency to become normalised in the nascent sector.

The next recommendation was again for agencies and data providers, stating that *ESG ratings and data products providers could consider adopting and implementing written policies and procedures designed to help ensure their decisions are independent, free from political or economic interference, and appropriately address potential conflicts of interest that may arise from, among other things, the ESG ratings and data products providers' organisational structure, business or financial activities, or the financial interests of the ESG ratings and ESG data products providers and their officers and employees.* One of the most important issues here is the need to inject *perceived* independence into the sector. This is because if the ESG rating space is to meet the requirements of the growing investment pool that will need to utilise the ratings of the ESG rating agencies, then having that perceived independence is a non-negotiable. Whether or not they need to be actually independent is another matter entirely and something we will cover in the last chapter, but the perception is all-important. IOSCO were aware that conflicts of interest, given the unique and rapidly evolving nature of the ESG rating marketplace is something that will be inherent to the nascent industry, as subsidiaries sit within much more influential parents, and as ESG rating agencies position themselves within a much more subjective data stream than credit rating agencies ever have.

The next recommendation is that *ESG ratings and data products providers could consider identifying, avoiding or appropriately managing, mitigating and disclosing potential conflicts of interest that may compromise the independence and objectivity of the ESG rating and ESG data products provider's operations.* The alignment here is noted in the report and further emphasises IOSCO's understandings of the underlying dynamics of the ESG rating space.

In seeking to set standards in relation to transparency from the very beginning of the regulatory journey for the ESG rating space, the next recommendation states that *ESG ratings and data products providers could consider making adequate levels of public disclosure and transparency a priority for their ESG ratings and data products, including their methodologies and processes to enable the users of the product to understand what the product is and how it is produced, including any potential conflicts of interest and while maintaining a balance with respect to proprietary or confidential information, data and methodologies.* What is clear here – as IOSCO provides guidelines for the ESG rating agencies that range from clearly labelling their products and providing explainers, to publicly disclosing data sources – is that the lessons from the credit rating world are at the forefront of the thinking. Underlying data sources, combined with methodological transparency, were key symptoms of an underlying problem in the credit rating space, and by insisting on the promotion of transparency, the message from IOSCO to national regulators and legislators is that base standards in relation to transparency should be established immediately.

The intricacies of the ESG rating space are identified in the report. The prevalence for the investor-pays model means that the connection between the issuer and the ESG rating agency is not, necessarily, present like it would be in the issuer-pays-dominated credit rating space. Having that access to incentivise issuers is one of the key selling points to the issuer-pays compensation model, but there are also the contractual underpinnings which protect the transmission of sensitive data. Without that contractual underpinning, IOSCO suggests with its next recommendation that *ESG ratings and data products providers could consider adopting and implementing written policies and procedures designed to address and protect all non-public information received from or communicated to them by any entity, or its agents, related to their ESG ratings and data products, in a manner appropriate in the circumstances.* This is extremely important for a variety of reasons. One is that even legally developed jurisdictions will not have the necessary coverage of the transmission of sensitive non-financial information like they may have for sensitive financial information, so until that legal infrastructure is adequately erected, written procedures that can provide a level of certainty would be a good start in the ESG rating space.

The report then turns its attentions to the 'users' of the ESG ratings. Drawing on the responses to the consultative process, IOSCO states that it understands that the variety of uses for ESG ratings and ESG data, in impacting aspects such as indices or ESG-related investment products as just two examples, means that a one-size-fits-all approach to protecting users of ESG rating agencies would not be possible. Therefore, rather than set forth rules that regulators and legislators should implement to protect users, IOSCO begins by suggesting that users themselves should enact processes to protect themselves in the new marketplace. *Market participants could consider conducting due diligence, or gathering and reviewing information on the ESG ratings and data products that they use in their internal processes. This due diligence or information-gathering and review could include an understanding of what is being rated or assessed by the product, how it is being rated or assessed, and limitations and the purposes for which the product is being used.* Clearly, this is meant to be supplemented by the other recommendations that focus on the ESG rating agencies developing their own processes in terms of transparency, so that such due diligence on behalf of users could be made possible.

The report then focuses on the relationship between ESG rating agencies (and data providers) and issuers as the last critical pillar of the space. They start by recommending that *ESG ratings and data products providers could consider improving information-gathering processes with entities covered by*

their products in a manner that leads to more efficient information procure-
ment for both the providers and these entities, and quickly follow this up with
the recommendation that, *where feasible and appropriate, ESG ratings and*
data products providers could consider responding to and addressing issues
flagged by entities covered by their ESG ratings and data products while
maintaining the objectivity of these products. To provide context to these
recommendations, IOSCO continues by describing approaches that ESG rating
agencies may take, including 'communicating in advance when they expect to
request this information [from the issuer] regarding their ESG ratings and data
products', and that where possible the ESG rating agencies could pre-populate
questionnaires with publicly available information for the issuers to review.
This could help, although as we heard from issuers responding to the *Rate the*
Raters report, reviewing the ESG rating agencies' interpretation of publicly
available documentation has proven to be quite difficult and time-consuming.
IOSCO finishes this advice to issuers and ESG rating agencies by suggesting
that the ESG rating agencies could 'provide a clear and consistent contact point
with whom the covered entity can interact to address any queries relating to
the assessment', and also informing the issue of the grounds of an ESG rating
before publication whilst also ensuring that enough time is given for the issuer
to respond.

The last recommendation of the report – namely that *entities subject to*
assessment by ESG ratings and data products providers could consider
streamlining their disclosure processes for sustainability-related information
to the extent possible, bearing in mind jurisdictions' applicable regulatory
and other legal requirements – is a slight misnomer in that the push for sustainability-related disclosure has its own momentum and will certainly not be
affected by this recommendation. Issuers will not be meeting their obligations
to report on sustainability to make things easier for ESG rating agencies,
but to meet the ever-growing demand of regulators, legislators, and society
moreover.

Those ten recommendations are, one quickly finds, rather bland. There is
nothing particularly revolutionary in them, and they mirror closely the safest
components of the credit rating regulatory developments witnessed in the
aftermath of the GFC. However, to focus on this understanding is to entirely
misunderstand the global regulatory processes within the financial sector.
IOSCO's recommendations are simply that, and they are not binding on
anybody. What they exist to do is to give national authorities the justification
to get things moving within their inner machinery, like the deployment of
resources, funds, and expertise to meet a certain regulatory challenge. By
harnessing the academic and industry viewpoints, IOSCO starts the official
ball rolling, and that is exactly what has happened. What follows is a collection

of accounts from around the world, in no particular order, to demonstrate the current state of the need to bring order to the nascent industry of ESG ratings.

4.2 The European Union

On 13 June 2023, after a substantial consultative period, the European Commission launched its proposed Regulation of ESG Rating Agencies and Data Providers.[35] The proposal makes clear that it does not sit in isolation, but rather as an integral component of the wider European Sustainable Finance Strategy that was launched and adopted in 2021. After some preamble, which mostly revolves around the key declaration that 'the current ESG rating market suffers from deficiencies and is not functioning properly, with investors and rated entities' needs regarding ESG ratings are not being met and confidence in ratings is being undermined', the proposal moves on to the underpinnings of the newly proposed Regulation. Yet, before we move on, it is worth noting that the proposed Regulation is accompanied by a detailed impact assessment.[36] The impact assessment covers critical issues, ranging from the legal and policy context of the proposed Regulation to the variety of problems the proposed Regulation seeks to remedy and the variety of potential impacts on key stakeholders.

The first key piece of information that is included in the proposed Regulation is the estimation of the costs. The European Commission (EC) suggests that no more than 20 full-time employees should be needed from ESMA, the chosen regulator, to oversee the implementation and oversight of this new Regulation, for a total cost of €3.7–3.8 million a year. This cost is to be met by the 59 entities the EC has identified as being prospectively captured by the Regulation in the form of supervisory fees, although there is proportion injected into that proposed scheme for smaller providers. ESMA is selected as it is the obvious choice, both because of its position as chief regulator of credit rating activities in the bloc, but also because of its centrality amongst the many member states' 'competent authorities', who would all have to coalesce to meet the regulatory objectives of the proposed Regulation.

However, it is now important to work through the proposed Regulation, article by article. It is important because the proposed Regulation bucks the trend in being entirely predictable and offers almost revolutionary aspects to the field of regulating rating-based activities. Because of this, there is a high likelihood that the lobbying efforts from affected entities will be great, because key revenue streams are threatened under the proposed Regulation, as we shall see. The Regulation begins in Article 2 by affirming the scope of the proposed Regulation, stating that the Regulation would not apply to: private ESG ratings which are not intended for public disclosure; the provision of raw ESG data not intended for ratings; credit ratings captured under the 2009

Regulation; 'second-party opinions' on sustainability bonds; and private ESG ratings produced by central banks. There are issues with this list, however, because aspects such as 'second-party opinions' (SPOs) can carry weight, are utilised by the market (from issuers seeking to add further authority to a prospective bond sale), and as the book will eventually conclude, are a signalling component of the ESG rating agency from which they would derive income and profit. It is therefore disappointing that this was not included in the scope of the Regulation, although it is understandable because, in the credit rating arena, SPOs are similarly outside of the regulatory perimeter around the world.

Article 3 provides definitions, whilst Article 4 declares that any legal person who wishes to provide ESG ratings inside of the EU shall be subject to ESMA's oversight. Article 5 builds on this and puts forward a system of registration that ESMA will oversee, much like that in the credit rating space. Annex I contains all of the necessary information that an applicant would need, and the Regulation instructs ESMA to develop draft regulatory technical standards to accompany the information required in the Annex. Article 5 blends into Article 6, which breaks down the particular details of the structure of application, like the fact that ESMA must assess whether the application is complete within 30 days of receipt, and within 120 days come to a final decision on whether the application is successful or not, and provide reasons why if not. Articles 7 and 8 grant ESMA the powers to grant or refuse applications, and also to withdraw or suspend the licence of an ESG rating agency once registered.

Article 9 deals with perhaps one of the biggest issues facing the European regulation of the ESG rating space, and that is the question of *equivalence*. With the very largest ESG rating agencies being headquartered outside of the European Union, as we saw earlier thanks to the *Rate the Raters* report, the issue of regulating third-country-based entities is of critical importance. To meet that challenge, Article 9 spells out that if a third-country ESG rating provider wishes to provide services within the EU, it must only do so when it has first registered with ESMA, and also meets the conditions of being a legal person, registered in their home country as an ESG rating provider, and is subject to supervision in their own country. The entity must also ensure that the details of the relevant 'competent authority' in their own country are submitted, and the EU must recognise that country. This is problematic because, for the most part, no other country has ESG rating-related regulations! To that end, it is likely that flexibility will be injected here by ESMA to recognise the breadth of regulatory exposure from, say, MSCI as being adequate to count as under the requirement for equivalence. However, the proposed Regulation does declare that 'the Commission shall take into account whether the legal framework and supervisory practice of a third country ensures compliance with the IOSCO recommendations for ESG Ratings published in November 2021'; again, this is interesting because the USA, as just one example, has not formally put anything in place in line with the IOSCO recommendations, despite being the home of the most influential players in the nascent market. To perhaps get around this problem, Article 10 declares that 'an ESG rating provider located in the Union and authorised in accordance with Article 7 may endorse ESG ratings provided by a third country ESG rating provider belonging to the same group'. Subsidiarisation will likely therefore be the key to allowing the largest third-country providers entry into the bloc, as EU-based subsidiaries will effectively vouch for their third-country parents, whilst containing liability at the same time.

Article 11 provides some base standards for third-country providers and their access to the European marketplace, whereas Article 12 covers cooperation arrangements between ESMA and competent authorities in third countries. Article 13 sets out the details of a register of information that can be included on the European Single Access Point (ESAP), before Article 14 sets out the 'general principles' that apply to ESG rating agencies, which clearly form the nucleus of the Regulation's proposed impact:

1. ESG rating providers shall ensure the independence of their rating activities, including from all political and economic influences or constraints.
2. ESG rating providers shall have in place rules and procedures that ensure that their ESG rating are provided and published or made available in accordance with this Regulation.
3. ESG rating providers shall employ systems, resources and procedures that are adequate and effective to comply with their obligations under this Regulation.
4. ESG rating providers shall adopt and implement written policies and procedures that ensure that their ESG ratings are based on a thorough analysis of all relevant information available to them.
5. ESG rating providers shall adopt and implement internal due diligence policies and procedures that ensure that their business interests do not impair the independence or accuracy of the assessment activities.
6. ESG rating providers shall adopt and implement sound administrative and accounting procedures, internal control mechanisms, and effective control and safeguard arrangements for information processing systems.
7. ESG rating providers shall use rating methodologies for the ESG ratings they provide that are rigorous, systematic, objective and capable of validation and shall apply those rating methodologies continuously.
8. ESG rating providers shall review the rating methodologies referred to in paragraph 6 on an on-going basis and at least annually.
9. ESG rating providers shall monitor and evaluate the adequacy and effectiveness of the systems, resources and procedures referred to in paragraph 2 at least annually and take appropriate measures to address any deficiencies.
10. ESG rating providers shall establish and maintain a permanent and effective oversight function to ensure oversight of all aspects of the provision of their ESG ratings. ESG rating providers shall develop and maintain robust procedures regarding their oversight function.
11. ESG rating providers shall adopt, implement, and enforce measures to ensure that their ESG ratings are based on a thorough analysis of all the information

that is available to them and that is relevant to their analysis in accordance with their rating methodologies. They shall adopt all necessary measures to ensure that the information they use in assigning ESG ratings is of sufficient quality and from reliable sources. ESG rating providers shall explicitly mention that their ESG ratings are their own opinion.

12. ESG rating providers shall not disclose information about their intellectual capital, intellectual property, know-how or the results of innovation that would qualify as trade secrets as defined in Article 2, point (1), of Directive (EU) 2016/943 of the European Parliament and of the Council.

13. ESG rating providers shall only make changes to their ESG ratings in accordance with their rating methodologies published pursuant to Article 21.

These principles are clearly in line with the recommendations from IOSCO. Basic tenets of transparency, governance, and essentially the formalisation of rating in the ESG sector are all now embedded into the law within the EU, at least in a proposed fashion. There is nothing too radical here, apart from the fact that the Regulation proposes to mandate these standards through a legal mechanism.

Yet, the next article certainly is radical. Article 15 simply states that ESG rating providers shall not provide any of the following activities:

(a) consulting activities to investors or undertakings;
(b) the issuance and sale of credit ratings;
(c) the development of benchmarks;
(d) investment activities;
(e) audit activities;
(f) banking, insurance, or reinsurance activities.

On the face of it, and judging by initial reaction in the rating community, subsection (a) is extraordinarily radical. Even my own doctoral thesis[37] and first monograph[38] called distinctly for the prohibition of ancillary services in the rating sector (with a focus on credit ratings), and after including it in my submission to the European Commission, it seems the idea has taken hold. Yet, on closer inspection, that may not be the case.

To ban an ESG rating agency from providing credit ratings make sense, as does prohibiting the development of benchmarks, investment activities, audit activities, and banking, insurance, and reinsurance activities. That all makes sense. But, does banning providing *investors* with consultancy services make any sense? Returning to my own doctoral thesis for one moment, the entire thesis was focused on proving that the provision of ancillary services from a credit rating was an example of economic rent-taking, meaning that the agencies did not *need* to provide the service, but did so to extract the maximum amount of resources from their privileged position. The thesis's main argument was that the revenues from ancillary services fundamentally blunted any form of acceptable punishment, with the analysis being that only financial punishments (in the form of settlements) were deemed systemically acceptable, as proved to be the case in 2015 and 2017; the profits from the provision of ancillary services dwarfed the 'record' settlements achieved by the DoJ. Yet, that thesis was based on the identification of a clear conflict of interest between the credit rating agencies and issuers, who were paying for the ratings. Whilst it is true that the same conflict of interest could apply to the investor-pays model, whereby the investor may apply pressure for better ratings to be attributed to entities so that they can invest in them, that risk is fundamentally lower in the investor-pays model than it is for issuer-pays. What the prohibition actually does is prevent investors from onboarding advice on how to best understand the ESG ratings, which as we know are very subjective and complex in nature. This could be problematic for the nascent industry and, I would presume, will be one of the loudest arguments put forward by ESG rating agencies and key investors in the intervening period for consultation on the proposed Regulation.

Article 16 deals with the conflicts of interest that may reveal themselves within the agencies, like between rating analysts and those with commercial interests. It does not, however, as no regulator has ever done, address the problematic 'rating committee' that sits at the final stage of the rating's journey. In the credit rating space, the rating committee is also considered 'out of bounds' from a regulatory perspective, though the documentation that supports a rating committee is stored and made available for regulatory examination, with the results being anonymously codified for the regulatory reports of the relevant regulator. In the ESG rating space, there will be no rules affirmed that declare that senior leaders within the ESG rating agency cannot be in the room to monitor, influence, or even intimidate analysts to come to the right decision *commercially*. It is understood why this has not been tackled by the Regulation – because any perceived intervention by the regulator into the *perceived independence* of an (ESG) rating agency is unacceptable systemically speaking – but to not even have it referenced is also disappointing.

Articles 17–20 cover procedural elements within the ESG rating agency, focusing on aspects such as record-keeping (17), complaints-handling mechanisms (18), and preventing outsourcing of critical elements of the inner workings of an ESG rating agency (19). Article 20 covers some of the potential exemptions from meeting such governance requirements that can be obtained, usually based upon size and scale. Article 21, however, is where the Regulation starts to inject key details regarding the inner processes of the ESG rating agencies, all with a crucial caveat. Jumping ahead slightly, Article 26 confirms bluntly:

> In carrying out their duties under this Regulation, ESMA, the Commission or any public authorities of a Member State shall not interfere with the content of ESG ratings or methodologies.

There is a very important reason why the Regulation is attempting to establish this principle in law. The Commission is acutely aware that there needs to be a balance with regards to regulating the sector, because while injecting authority is positive and clearly needed, the underlying dynamics of the concept of rating mean that nothing is more important than the perceived independence of the agency. The Commission, in seeking to make changes to aspects such as the methodological processes, and how the agencies manage the inherent conflicts of interests, must do so with extreme caution, and it clearly believes that Article 26, in outwardly constraining the activities of ESMA, will be enough to provide the security the system needs.

This all makes sense when we understand the aims of Article 21 and what comes after it. Article 21 instructs ESG rating agencies to publicly disclose their rating methodologies, models, and key rating assumptions, and that ESMA shall concoct regulatory technical standards against which the ESG rating agencies must disclose these details. This will be the first time that many ESG rating agencies will have ever made their methodological processes public, so the technical standards will be an important addition to the field by ESMA. Furthermore, Article 22 instructs ESG rating agencies to make particular information from Annex III available to subscribers and rated entities, which is the Annex that includes all of the disclosure requirements ranging from the scientific evidence and assumptions that underpin ratings, whether the rating is backward- or forward-looking, potential shortcomings of the rating, policies for revision, and the weighting between factors (amongst a range of other aspects to be disclosed).

Article 23 covers the internal governance of the agencies, and insists upon there being in place robust governance agreements which can be translated and transmitted to the public. The sentiment of the article, in describing very broad situations that the ESG rating agencies must consider ahead of time, is to provide ESMA with the flexibility to govern on the issue of internal governance because the scope is so wide that any identified conflicts of interest that materialise should have, by order of the article at least, been protected against. To complete the approach, the article declares that 'ESG rating providers shall disclose to ESMA all existing or potential conflicts of interests, including conflicts of interest arising from the ownership or control of the ESG rating providers'. In terms of protecting against conflicts that may impact or emanate from employees, Article 24 insists that those involved in ratings have to have the relevant skillsets and be subjected to effective management and supervision, not be subject to undue influence, be properly compensated so as not to create conflicts of interests or perverse incentives, and be prohibited from engaging in commercial work on behalf of the agency, including being subjected to efficient informational control procedures to prevent sharing that could amount to conflicts of interest. Lastly in this chapter of articles, Article 25 confirms that ESG rating agencies should charge users appropriately for the given rating.

Chapter 4 of the proposed Regulation focuses on the regulatory procedures that will affect the ESG rating sector. We have covered the fact that Article 26 prevents ESMA from interfering in the methodologies of the agencies, and Articles 27 and 28 cover the requirement for ESMA to produce an annual report on the sector like they do for the credit rating agencies, and that each member state shall designate a 'competent authority' to liaise with ESMA on the task of implementing the ESG rating Regulation, as is also the case in the credit rating sector. Articles 30, 31, and 32 are all based upon Article 29, which says ESMA shall not require disclosure of information that is subject to legal privilege, with those articles focusing on the requirement of ESG rating agencies and associated entities to furnish ESMA with information required to effectively regulate the sector (30), and that ESMA may conduct general investigations which may involve the examination of records (31) via on-site inspections (32).

Article 33 details the range of sanctions that ESMA may give to registered entities, including: withdrawal of registration; temporary prohibition of the ability to provide ESG ratings broadly; suspension of registration; requirement to cease particular operations to bring identified infringements to an end; imposing fines; and issuing public notices. Article 34 details the scope of the fines applicable, with the maximum amount being 10% of 'the total annual net turnover of the ESG rating provider', though this can be capped by subsidiarisation. Article 35 provides ESMA with the option to impose 'periodic penalty payments' to stop particular actions, and Article 36 instructs ESMA to publicly disclose every fine or periodic penalty payment that it apportions. Articles 37, 38, and 39 cover the procedural rules to ESMA taking supervisory measures and imposing fines (37), and the processes available to penalised parties (38), including the purview of the Court of Justice as the final arbiter if required (39). The remaining articles are brief and without much detail, but include the supervisory fees that ESMA can charge (40), the delegation of tasks that ESMA can attribute to competent authorities (41), how they exchange information (42), and how ESMA may deal with notifications and suspension requests from competent authorities (43), with Article 44 confirming that the obligation of professional secrecy applies to all regulatory bodies concerned.

Article 45 covers the exercise and revocation of the delegation and objections to delegated Acts, Article 46 covers any amendments to the Annexes, and Article 47 the committee procedure within the European Commission. Article 48 covers any transitional provisions in terms of the latest ESG rating agencies must register with ESMA, Article 49 promises a review after five years of the Regulation being enacted, and finally Article 50 covers the date that the Regulation will enter into force and apply, with the only details at this early stage being that the Regulation will 'apply' no later than six months after it comes into force.

On reflection, we can see an attempt to regulate the ESG rating industry that both falls in line with IOSCO recommendations and standard practice in the credit rating sector, but also in parts really pushes against the boundaries of what is acceptable, usually, when regulating a rating sector. The suggestion that ancillary services will be outlawed is extremely radical, but comes with important caveats. The effect of providing ancillary services in the ESG rating sector is very different from that in the credit rating sector, and prohibiting it actually causes potential harm to the users of the ESG ratings, whereas prohibition in the credit rating sector would actually benefit the 'users', with users being identified in both cases as investors. Even though I have spent a large part of my career campaigning for the dissolution of ancillary services in the credit rating sector, I think the prohibition proposed in this Regulation will be reversed or reduced, and that it is probably right that this is done; preventing investors from being able to purchase assistance from the ESG rating agencies on how to utilise their ratings most effectively is potentially harmful to the development of the sector, especially given the reduced risk of applying pressure that the investor-pays model brings in comparison with the issuer-pays model.

Other than that, the proposed Regulation is arguably quite bland. It insists upon base standards as suggested by IOSCO, but makes the conscious attempt to stand well clear of any insinuation that they are attempting to interfere in the development of ratings, as they must. However, there is no mention of holding particular parts of the rating process to account, which is something they can do. By this I mean that there is no mention of the rating committees, or of empowering ESMA to publicise any issues that it fines. In the credit rating sector, both ESMA and the SEC in the US conduct on-site inspections and examine documents that the public will never see, but in their annual reports they anonymise the results, often only declaring that 'a large' credit rating agency infringed upon this or that, or a 'small' credit rating agency. There is no mention of forcing ESMA to do anything different from this, which is a massively missed opportunity, because the regulator will undoubtedly take the same approach and the public will be none the wiser about material breaches of law that the regulator smooths over before the matter becomes public.

There is also no reference to liability, which unsurprisingly for this book is a major issue. We know that in the credit rating sector the issue of liability is a very treacherous one for legislators, but they have at least tried to influence proceedings; in relation to ESG ratings, there is no such reference. This is problematic: waiting for liability issues to arise is a fool's errand, because legislators will have to address it at some point. If it takes the ESG rating agencies to cause great harm to the sector in order for the legislators to address it, citizens who will be affected will have every right to question why the Commission refused to address it when setting the base standards. Even if the approach was to set the incredibly high bar that exists in the credit rating regulations, that would still be an improvement on saying nothing at all. Obviously national courts will take the credit rating regulations into account if there is ever a case brought against an ESG rating agency, but the fact that those rules apply to a completely different industry will make comparisons weak at best.

Nevertheless, despite these issues, the proposed Regulation is still a massive jump forward in the story of the ESG rating agencies. Parts of the proposed Regulation may look onerous for ESG rating agencies, but the reality is that it is all positive for them, because the formality that the Regulation brings to the sector is unmatched. The era of the ESG rating agency in Europe will be under way when this Regulation is approved, in whatever shape or form. Elsewhere that process of formalising the ESG rating industry is at different stages, but, as we shall see, it is all moving in one direction.

4.3   India

Whilst the European developments are taking centre stage in the formalising of the ESG rating space, it is actually India that has acted first and formally begun the regulation of the ESG rating space. The Credit Rating Regulations of 1999 were amended with effect from 4 July 2023 to now prescribe guidelines for the registration of ESG rating agencies, general obligations, and processes related to inspecting the agencies. On top of this, a code of conduct was brought in to bring about a set of base standards for the industry operating in India. However, in order to assist with the understanding of the rules, a 'Master Circular' was produced and disseminated on 12 July 2023, and it is that document which is worth reviewing.[39]

The Circular starts by confirming that SEBI (the Securities and Exchange Board of India) will be the regulator tasked with monitoring the ESG rating space in India, just as it does for the credit rating agencies operating within the jurisdiction. That confirmation leads into a similar system to that in the EU, where ESG rating agencies will have to register with SEBI as an ESG rating provider and through that registration process provide a host of details and agree to be subject to SEBI's authority. Yet, whilst the EU was abundantly cautious in relation to involving itself in the processes of the ESG rating agencies, the Indian regime is markedly different. For example, an early declaration in relation to rating scales and clarity for market participants tells us that 'in the interest of clarity to market participants, it is mandated that ESG ratings shall be provided on a scale of 0–100, where 100 represents the maximum score'. How this will work in reality we do not yet know, because more established players who have subsidiaries and formal partnerships in the country have their own distinctive scales which are universally recognised.

Interestingly, the Indian ruling does interject with regards to business model, which the EU proposed Regulation does not. It states that ESG rating agencies can use the investor- or issuer-pays business models, of course, but that they cannot mix them to form a hybrid business model. For example, 'in order to mitigate potential conflicts of interest, it is mandated that ERPs shall not follow a hybrid business model, i.e. an ERP shall not assign certain ESG rating based on issuer-pay model, while assigning another ESG rating based on a subscriber-pays business model'. This is interesting not only for the fact that it dictates which model can be used, but in that it rightly identifies the potential evolution of the marketplace. The European model simply ignores the chances of processes and approaches changing in the ESG rating space, which is problematic. For instance, there is every chance that ESG rating agencies, once their business becomes more formalised, will move towards charging issuers to have their position and products rated, at which point in Europe the prohibition on ancillary service provision, as just one example, will become obsolete because it only applies to investors. In India, ESG rating agencies must commit to one or the other, and confirm this.

The Indian model is closely aligned to the proposed EU model, simply because it makes sense and follows both accepted international approaches, but also because they are closely aligned to the recommendations put forward by IOSCO (because IOSCO drives regulatory movement). So, the Indian rules on aspects such as methodological transparency, record-keeping, and publishing aspects such as material changes to methodologies and approaches, are all evident and present. There is also the requirement, like in the EU, to explain one's ratings and provide the marketplace with the associated support for the underlying data that made up a given rating. What is really interesting, however, is that the Circular details, extensively, the guidelines for both an investor- and issuer-pays business model, providing legal boundaries which will govern the two relationships.

After listing the disclosures that ESG rating agencies must make, ranging from rating histories to comparable data on their websites, the Circular moves to the question of internal audits. Rather than having the regulator make annual examinations of the ESG rating agencies to fall in line with practices from around the world, Indian ESG rating agencies (just like credit rating agencies) must be audited by external and independent professionals once a year. The Circular gives details of what that audit must contain, and how independent the auditor must be, i.e., they must have been operating for more than three years, and be able to evidence that they have had no commercial relationship with the rating agency, other than to audit. The Circular ends by declaring that appropriate firewalls must be erected between the rating agencies and their associate businesses, as an extra attempt to reduce the impact of conflicts of interest.

The Indian approach is extensive and contextualised for the Indian experience. Western agencies are not dominant in India, but do own stakes in the largest Indian agencies, like CRISIL, which was purchased by S&P in 2005. Also, India has a very different constitution from places like the US, for example, where India has many more SMEs, which brings about a different way of rating. This is why the Indian regulatory development can afford to push for changes to particular methodological processes, for example, because western agencies will not be too affected. Irrespective of the nuanced differences, it is India that has leapt from the traps first and formally regulated the ESG rating space. In other jurisdictions, the process is taking either a different or a slower trajectory.

4.4   Japan

On 15 December 2022, Japan's Financial Services Agency (FSA) launched its response to the IOSCO call. If you can remember, the IOSCO calls suggested that a formal regulatory structure should be erected, or instead a code of conduct should be established in league with the ESG rating space in one's jurisdiction. In Japan, the decision so far has been to go down the latter route, and the Code of Conduct for ESG Evaluation and Data Providers was published in December.[40] The Code is made up of six distinct principles, all of which have context added, and one piece of guidance for investors and one piece of guidance for companies in association with the Code.

The first principle states that *ESG evaluation and data providers should strive to ensure the quality of ESG evaluation and data they provide. The basic procedures necessary for this purpose should be established.* The guidelines associated with this principle suggest that methodologies should be applied consistently across the agencies' businesses, and that there should be regular checks for discrepancies between the evaluation results and the methodologies that underpin them. Interestingly, the Code makes clear that the role of the ESG rating agency is not to check on the accuracy of the underlying data disclosed from companies, saying that is the responsibility of the companies themselves.

The second principle says that *ESG evaluation and data providers should secure necessary professional human resources to ensure the quality of the evaluation and data provision services they provide, and should develop their own professional skills.* In association with this principle, the Code states that agencies should ensure that analysts have the appropriate knowledge to complete the task of developing ratings, and that the agencies should ultimately invest considerably in the human resources of their agency. The Code references the dearth of talent within the ESG rating space and suggests that building capacity internally will be the best way to develop the space.

The third principle focuses on the management of conflicts of interests and instructs that *ESG evaluation and data providers should establish effective policies so that they can independently make decisions and appropriately address conflicts of interest that may arise from their organisation and ownership, business, investment and funding, and compensation for their officers and employees, etc. With regard to conflicts of interest, providers should identify their own activities and situations that could undermine the independence, objectivity, and neutrality of their business, and avoid potential conflicts of interest or appropriately manage and reduce the risk of conflict of interest.* Associated issues that the Code identifies with regards to conflicts of interest include developing questionnaires robustly but fairly to avoid forcing an entity to engage with paid ancillary services just to adequately complete the questionnaire, but also include developing appropriate compensation structures. This is accentuated by discussion associated with the principle, in which it is stated that 'with regards to independence, it is necessary to pay attention to both the independence of the company and that of the employees such as analysts', with the inference being that appropriate firewalls between analysts and commercial endeavours are required.

Principle four is concerned with transparency, stating that *ESG evaluation and data providers should recognise that ensuring transparency is an essential and prioritised issue, and publicly clarify their basic approach in providing services, such as the purpose and basic methodology of evaluations. Methodologies and processes for formulating services should be sufficiently disclosed.* This falls in line with the widespread calls for the methodologies and the methodological processes employed within agencies to be made public, and the guidelines to this principle call for agencies to provide supportive data and explanations to publicly available ratings so that users can best navigate them and understand them. The Code also calls for the underlying data to be explained for the user, so that estimated data is classified as such so that users can understand what underpins a rating, for example. Additionally, the Code calls for these processes to be updated and conveyed to the public, so that any methodological changes are publicly explained so that users can be aware of the material effects of such changes.

The fifth principle states that *ESG evaluation and data providers should establish policies and procedures to appropriately protect non-public information obtained in the course of business.* The focus here is on protecting the informational flow into and through the agency, so that any confidential or sensitive information that comes from companies or issuers is protected, resulting in an increased trust in the process. The final principle focuses again on the informational flow, stating that *ESG evaluation and data providers should devise and improve the way they gather information from companies so that the process becomes efficient for both service providers and companies or necessary information can be sufficiently obtained. When important or reasonable issues related to information source are raised by companies subject to evaluation, ESG evaluation and data providers should appropriately respond to the issues.* The guidelines to this principle make clear that the processes of collecting data must become more streamlined and focused more on the experience of the target company. For example, there is mention of the need to give more warning when requesting data, established dedicated contacts for the companies, giving the companies time to adequately respond to any issues in the interpretation of the data, and providing adequate pathways for companies to complain.

Interestingly, the Code ends with two recommendations: one for investors and one for issuers/companies. With respect to investors, the Code recommends:

> Investors should carefully examine and understand the purpose, methodologies, and limitations of ESG evaluation and data they utilize for their investment decisions. When there are issues in the evaluation results, they should engage in dialogue with ESG evaluation and data providers or companies. In addition, investors should publicly clarify the basic approach of how they utilize ESG evaluation and data in their investment decisions.

In addition to this recommendation, the Code suggests that investors (especially institutional investors) should seek to publicly disclose how they incorporate the ESG ratings into their investment decision-making processes, in an attempt to essentially bring about what the European Union is attempting to bring about with its taxonomy (albeit on a substantially smaller scale). For companies and issuers, the Code recommends that *companies should disclose ESG information in an easy-to-understand manner, taking into account regulatory and other updates.* Again, this is a very short interjection that reminds one of the CSRD, albeit substantially smaller in scale.

Ultimately, the so-called 'soft' approach that a code of conduct represents is demonstrated in the text of the Code. It is all very facilitative of the ESG rating agencies maintaining the current cultural practices whilst meeting the base standards suggested by the IOSCO final report. The final recommendations to investors and companies are slightly uncomfortable in that they mean very little and will not affect the trajectory of those two critical sectors of the economy in any way, and are placed at the end of the Code in an almost throw-away manner. Nevertheless, the base standards positioned in the IOSCO recommendations are at least represented in this Code of Conduct. Elsewhere, the decision on how to proceed is still being taken.

4.5   The United Kingdom

The United Kingdom is currently, at the time of writing (mid-July 2023), very much at the planning stage of how it will be responding to the call from IOSCO. On 22 November 2022, the Financial Conduct Authority (FCA) announced that it was forming a working group, co-chaired by M&G, Moody's, London Stock Exchange Group, and Slaughter and May, that would come together to develop a new code of conduct for ESG rating agencies.[41] The International Capital Market Association (ICMA) and the International Regulatory Strategy Group (ISRG) will be the secretariat that ultimately leads the work. The proposed code will focus on integrating the recommendations of IOSCO, and will likely look very similar to the Japanese code, albeit with contextualisation for the British marketplace. However, the code is expected to be a holding card whilst the UK Treasury decides whether it would like to press ahead with formal regulation.

On 30 March 2023, the UK government, via the Treasury, published a consultative document entitled *Future Regulatory Regime for Environmental, Social, and Governance (ESG) Ratings Providers.*[42] The consultation, which lasted from 30 March to 30 June 2023, reviewed a number of issues in its preamble and referenced the regulatory developments that this chapter has discussed as a key indicator of the movement of travel in the ESG rating space. Ultimately, the Treasury declare that the key rationale for considering regulation is that 'HM Treasury considers there is clear benefit to be gained from improving the transparency of methodologies, governance, and processes of ESG ratings providers. These outcomes could be brought about through regulation.' In order to determine whether that regulation was needed, and if so what it may entail, the document asked prospective participants a variety of questions. The questions ranged from the simple (do you agree that regulation should be introduced?) to the complex (in what way do investors use ESG rating agencies and when?) and everything else in between. The Treasury also sought to understand what exemptions may be needed to any future regulation, and whether and how proportionality should be injected into the regulatory endeavour.

The UK represents quite a unique case because it is very much subjected to an ever-evolving environment. Not that all countries are not also subjected to such volatile landscapes, but very few have just voluntarily left a major economic bloc to become more independent, all whilst containing one of the world's leading financial centres (as well legal centres). This unique situation the UK finds itself in presents significant challenges to the British government, but also significant opportunity. The balance-related question facing the UK at the moment revolves around creating an open business-friendly environment, on one hand, and not being perceived to be producing a regulatory race-to-the-bottom, on the other, just to secure investment and business. At the moment, the UK is struggling more than almost every other developed economy from an austere political environment which has magnified negative economic circumstances emanating from the pandemic and the Ukraine–Russia conflict. It is within this environment that the Treasury must make the right decision for Britain's future, because the proposed centrality of the ESG rating agencies in the coming decades means that getting it right now could pay huge dividends, but getting it wrong could cause lasting hardship. Yet, the decisions are being taken and eventually, I predict, the UK will formally regulate the ESG rating space, albeit likely in a much more facilitative manner than their European counterparts are currently proposing. On the other side of the Atlantic Ocean, however, things are not so developed.

4.6   The United States

The topics that have been discussed and analysed in this book are beginning to move to the forefront of thinking around the world, but for a variety of reasons the same issues are extremely contentious in the United States. One reason is that the concept of pushing business to do things in different ways is at odds with the American culture, one rooted in the concept of free enterprise and the corporation, and one that really consolidated the concept of the corporation seeking to prioritise the profit maximation of its shareholders above all else. On top of that cultural foundation, the US has seen the rise of particularly divisive politics in recent years, with key political and legal organs like the US Senate hamstrung by political division. It is from that foundation that the US faces the crucial questions facing humanity in the modern era.

With that in mind, there is remarkably very little to report for the jurisdiction that plays host to the majority of the largest ESG rating agencies and all of the largest credit rating agencies. The only development, relatively speaking, in terms of the informational flow we have considered in this book so far, is that on 21 March 2022, the SEC announced that it would be proposing a rule that would:

> require registrants to include certain climate-related disclosures in their registration statements and periodic reports, including information about climate-related risks that are reasonably likely to have a material impact on their business, results of operations, or financial condition and certain climate-related financial statement metrics in a note to their audited financial statements.[43]

The proposed rule[44] is relatively revolutionary in the US and has brought about high praise and even more criticism. The US is seemingly following a private-sector-led path, dominated by the ISSB principles we have already covered, which push a distinctly single-materiality pathway forward; the SEC's proposed rule pushes a similar single-materiality narrative, you may have noticed.

Whilst seemingly avoiding double materiality at all costs, even the concept of ESG is contentious in the US and is proving to be a central component in what many are referring to as the 'culture wars'. Central to this is the concept of ESG representing that which is 'woke', or virtue-signalling as others may refer to it. Nevertheless, the spotlight on ESG is quickly becoming political, and in many Republican-held states, ESG is under attack and with it so too are ESG rating agencies. In Florida, Governor Ron DeSantis has effectively banned Floridian institutional investors and those connected to the state government from utilising ESG ratings and ESG-related information, with DeSantis saying on the day he signed sweeping state-level legislation into force, 'we want them to act as fiduciaries. We do not want them engaged on these ideological joyrides.' Morningstar, the owner of DBRS, said in response to the understanding that credit rating agencies operating in the state would be unable to consult on ESG information, 'if we as a rating agency cannot assess environmental, social, or governance risk, that creates a problem for us. There are climate and weather risks that are highly relevant, especially in a state like Florida, and would be captured in our assessment of credit risk.'[45]

What is clear in the US is that not that much in relation to ESG is clear at all. Whilst there is evidence of progression, there is also plenty of evidence of regression. With the next presidential election taking place in 2024, and with it likely to consist of a Trump/Republican challenge to the Democrats in office, the future for the US and its relationship to the concept of ESG is very uncertain. Furthermore, there is no indication whatsoever that the US is considering meeting the call of IOSCO, which leaves the host of leading ESG rating agencies completely unregulated. There is certainly no right or wrong way in this field without answers, but the reality is that there is a growing divide with how different jurisdictions are choosing to tackle the issue of ESG ratings (or not).

5.   CONCLUSION

Understanding the ESG rating space was, as the title of the book suggests, critical for our understanding, and in this chapter we were introduced to the players in the space and the associated issues affecting the development of the industry. It was revealed that the nascent industry is not meeting the requirements of its users, and that if it were to do so, many fundamental processes within the industry would have to change. However, the issues affecting the industry are complex and nuanced, with many requiring a more specialised understanding more broadly. It is unlikely that such understanding will be forthcoming whilst the tabloid press continue to highlight inefficiencies without context, or the frustrations of billionaires negatively affected by the operational approaches of the industry continue to be given prevalence instead of contextualising approaches so that the public can at least understand the menu of operational approaches available.

Whilst one seriously doubts whether such books can ever become best-sellers and positively affect the general public's understanding of such financial matters (!), this book has endeavoured to at least inject the much-needed contextualisation into the discussion so that what at first may appear odd or antithetical can at least be understood, whether one agrees with it or not. For example, this chapter has shown an industry that has green shoots emanating from specialised forms of investing, but which has grown once some of the largest financial service providers entered the space. With large players like Bloomberg and MSCI competing for business with the credit rating oligopolists, it comes as no surprise to learn that some of the biggest M&A (mergers and acquisitions) deals in recent times have been for data-focused companies like S&P's takeover of IHS Markit for around $44 billion; as was suggested by the headline of a *Financial Times* article covering the story, perhaps 'data is the new oil'.[46]

Yet, we saw that there were serious issues with the form that the ESG rating industry has taken so far. The influence that oligopolistic behaviour is having in the space is starting to show, as early research suggests the takeovers that are happening are resulting in rating inflation for the commercial interests of the new parent companies.[47] Aside from this, there is a basic misunderstanding affecting the space that is causing real reputational damage in the public arena, as leading companies from seemingly pollutant-based or carcinogen-based industries are scoring high ESG rating scores, whilst others in more seemingly environmentally friendly industries are scoring much lower. This is solely because the differentiation between single and double materiality is not being transmitted to the public by way of educated discourse, but also because ESG rating agencies are not being as transparent as they should be with their methodological processes. There have been attempts from leading ESG rating CEOs to correct this misunderstanding, but it certainly is not concerted, whereas the approach in misinforming the public is certainly more concerted.

Whether one agrees that the ESG rating agencies should be utilising single or double materiality as their core focus is an important discussion, but a very different discussion. This is because the major ESG rating agencies, especially those that operate on a for-profit basis, have unilaterally decided to move the industry in that direction and there is no turning back; for those wanting a wholly double-materiality-based industry to flourish, one would have to start by making it profitable for the ESG rating agencies to deliver such a variant, which, at the moment, it is not. Part of the reason for this is that the ESG rating industry is slowly taking the shape of the credit rating sector, which is what is known as a 'natural oligopoly', one that is investor-driven. The same thing is revealing itself in the ESG rating space, with the requirements of investors needing to be met. It is the investors who, for the most part, want to know the *financial impact* of ESG, rather than the planetary effect of financial matters – until that changes, the ESG rating agencies will continue offering the paying investors what they want.

However, at the moment they are struggling to do that, no matter how hard they try. This is because, as we shall really get to understand in the next chapter, an investor-driven natural oligopoly operates on a small number of clear principles. One of those principles, for example, is the ability to utilise the ratings as signals, and those signals must be closely comparable to retain their authority as signals. At the moment, the ESG rating space is both too diverse, and the underpinning methodologies, interpretations, and approaches are too varied between raters. For an investor-driven marketplace, this is unacceptable. Too much 'noise' means the products cannot maximise their signalling power, and this is why the majority of the research on the sector, whether the researchers are conscious of this or not, is focusing on pushing for that divergence to stop, or at least massively reduce, so that the signalling power can reveal itself. The research is awash with references to 'divergence', 'commensurability', or a plethora of other terms which essentially reduce down to 'too many'.

The sheer pressure from investors, and then by association from issuers – who are all complaining of not being able to efficiently and effectively move resources in the ESG-related fields because of these issues – has led to a regulatory response. However, what we saw in the chapter was a global regulatory machine that said everything without saying the one thing they wanted or needed to say, and there is a direct reason for this. The regulatory regimes that have been adopted in India, proposed in Europe, voluntarily encouraged in Japan, and which are being consulted on in the UK all avoid the trap that post-GFC legislators fell into: mentioning the word 'competition'. It is interesting that despite all of the calls for more transparency, better and more observable training, and distinctive preventative measures for conflicts of interest, not one regulatory body has mentioned the word competition. There has been no mention of initiatives to improve competition, like rotating rating agencies, or providing an intermediary that could select rating agencies for issuances (like we saw after the GFC) because (a) increasing competition is not the issue this time, and (b) whilst a regulator can always discuss increasing competition, it can *never* discuss decreasing competition, even though, in this case, it is the answer to all of the industry's problems. It is for this reason that the regulatory initiatives that have begun are all very much soft to the touch, because taking the wrong decision now, regulatorily speaking, could have lasting and negative consequences that a regulator would not want to be associated with (think of the SEC still being criticised now for the NRSRO designation in 1975!).

What legislators and regulators can do, however, is apply base or minimum standards and then stand back. Things like enforcing centralised registration or enforcing methodological transparency will have no real positive effect on the industry, but they will avoid any negative effects, which, for the regulator had to be the main concern. Perhaps the main benefit from the ESG rating regulations and codes that have been developed is that the ESG rating space is becoming more formalised, which is perhaps the next stage of its journey. But, ultimately, something has to give if the agencies are to meet the distinctive demands of their user base, which for their part has been made abundantly clear: less noise. That need for less noise is not a polite request based on a wish, but a systemic need that is fundamental to the future flow of capital that is emanating from the growing ESG investment base, and it is a systemic need quite simply because the ESG rating agency has one role in the larger system – to produce signals.

NOTES

1.   James Hawley and Andrew Williams, 'The Emergence of Universal Owners: Some Implications of Institutional Equity Ownership' (2000) 43 Challenge 4, 43–61.
2.   Florian Berg, Julian F Koelbel, and Roberto Rigobon, 'Aggregate Confusion: The Divergence of ESG Ratings' (2019) MIT Sloan School Working Paper 5822-19, 5.
3.   Daniel Cash, *The Role of Credit Rating Agencies in Responsible Finance* (Palgrave Macmillan 2018).
4.   Aaron K. Chatterji, David I. Levine, and Michael W. Toffel, 'How Well do Social Ratings Actually Measure Corporate Social Responsibility?' [2009] 18 Journal of Economics & Management Strategy 1 125–169.
5.   Michael S Pagano, Graham Sinclair, and Tina Yang, 'Understanding ESG Ratings and ESG Indexes' in Sabri Boubaker, Douglas Cumming, and Duc K Nguyen, *Research Handbook of Finance and Sustainability* (Edward Elgar 2018) 340.
6.   For my own effort, see: Daniel Cash, *Sustainability Rating Agencies vs Credit Rating Agencies: The Battle to Serve the Mainstream Investor* (Palgrave Macmillan 2021).
7.   The SustainAbility Institute by ERM, *Rate the Raters 2023: ESG Ratings at a Crossroads* (2023) https://www.sustainability.com/globalassets/sustainability .com/thinking/pdfs/2023/rate-the-raters-report-april-2023.pdf.
8.   ibid 33.
9.   ibid 27.

10. S&P, *2023 CSA Methodology Updates* (2023) https://portal.csa.spglobal.com/survey/documents/CSA_2023_Methodology_Updates_Overview.pdf.

11. ESMA, *ESG Ratings: Status and Key Issues Ahead* (2021) https://www.esma.europa.eu/sites/default/files/trv_2021_1-esg_ratings_status_and_key_issues_ahead.pdf 107.

12. Giovanni Landi and Andrea Tomo, 'The Dark Side of Ethics in Finance: Empirical Evidences from the Italian Market' in Agata Stachowicz-Stanusch, Gianluigi Mangia, Adele Calarelli, and Wolfgang Amann, *Organisational Social Irresponsibility: Tools and Theoretical Insights* (IAP 2017) 164.

13. ibid 165.

14. Alice Wright, '"This is why ESG is the Devil": Elon Musk slams S&P's woke scores for giving Marlboro a HIGHER investment rating than Tesla – despite cigarettes being responsible for eight MILLION deaths a year' (2023) Daily Mail (Jun 14) https://www.dailymail.co.uk/news/article-12194317/Elon-Musk-slams-S-P-Global-ESG-scores-giving-Malboro-HIGHER-investment-rating-Tesla.html.

15. Colin Mayer, 'The research background to the final report of the Future of the Corporation programme on "Policy & Practice for Purposeful Business"' in Colin Mayer (ed), 'Foundations of the Future of the Corporate Programme Report "Policy & Practice for Purposeful Business"' (2022) 10 Journal of the British Academy 5, 10.

16. Henry A Fernandez, 'ESG Ratings: Setting the Record Straight' (2022) LinkedIn (Feb 4) https://www.linkedin.com/pulse/esg-ratings-setting-record-straight-henry-fernandez/.

17. Alex C Michalos, 'The Business Case for Asserting the Business Case for Business Ethics' (2013) 114 Journal of Business Ethics 4 599–606. 605.

18. CDP, *Annex to CDP Europe's Response to the Public Consultation on the Revision of the Non-Financial Reporting Directive* (2020) https://cdn.cdp.net/cdp-production/comfy/cms/files/files/000/003/445/original/CDP_response_to_public_consultation_on_revision_of_the_Non-Financial_Reporting_Directive.pdf.

19. Aaron K. Chatterji, David I. Levine, and Michael W. Toffel, 'How Well do Social Ratings Actually Measure Corporate Social Responsibility?' (2009) 18 Journal of Economics & Management Strategy 1 125–169, 127.

20. Pagano et al (n 5) 361.

21. Elena Escrig-Olmedo, Maria A Fernandez-Izquierdo, Idoya Ferrero-Ferrero, Juana M Rivera-Lirio and Maria J Munoz-Torres, 'Rating the Raters: Evaluating how ESG Rating Agencies Integrate Sustainability Principles' (2019) 11 Sustainability 915, 921.

22. ibid 1608.

23. Berg et al (n 2) 4.

24. ibid 19.

25. OECD, *OECD Business and Finance Outlook 2020 Sustainable and Resilient Finance* (OECD Publishing 2020) 28.

26. Berg et al (n 2) 28.

27. OECD (n 26) 29.

28. Escrig-Olmedo et al (n 22) 925.

29. Alfonso Del Giudice and Silvia Rigamonti, 'Does Audit Improve the Quality of ESG Scores? Evidence from Corporate Misconduct' (2020) 12 Sustainability 5670, 5682.

30. Fernando Garcia, Jairo Gonzalez-Bueno, Francisco Guijarro, and Javier Oliver, 'Forecasting the Environmental, Social, and Governance Rating of Firms by Using Corporate Financial Performance Variables: A Rough Set Approach' (2020) 12 Sustainability 8, 3324.

31. Natalie Runyon, 'The growing role of audit in ESG information integrity and assurance' (2022) Reuters (Oct 27) https:// www .thomsonreuters .com/ en -us/ posts/ tax -and -accounting/ esg -audit -integrity/ #: ~: text = CPAs %2C %20acting %20as %20auditors %2C %20have ,across %20the %20world %20has %20transpired.

32. Andrew Mountfield, Matthew Gardner, Bernd Kasemir, and Stephan Lienin, 'Integrated Management for Capital Markets and Strategy: The Challenges of "Value" Versus "Values" Sustainability Investment, Smart Bet, and their Consequences for Corporate Leadership' in Thomas Wunder, *Rethinking Strategic Management: Sustainable Strategizing for Positive Impact* (Springer 2019), 113.

33. IOSCO, *Environmental, Social and Governance (ESG) Ratings and Data Products Providers: Final Report* (2021) https://www.iosco.org/library/pubdocs/ pdf/IOSCOPD690.pdf.

34. ibid 7.

35. European Commission, *Proposal for a Regulation of the European Parliament and of the Council on the Transparency and Integrity of Environmental, Social, and Governance (ESG) Rating Activities* (2023) https:// ec .europa .eu/ info/ law/ better-regulation/ have -your-say/ initiatives/ 13330-Sustainable-finance -environmental-social-and-governance-ratings-and-sustainability-risks-in-credit -ratings_en.

36. European Commission, *Commission Staff Working Document: Impact Assessment Report* (2023) https://ec.europa.eu/finance/docs/law/230613-impact -assessment_en.pdf.

37. Daniel Cash, *The Regulation of Credit Rating Agencies: An Analysis of the Transgressions of the Rating Industry and a Measured Proposal for Reform* (2016) Durham e-Theses: http://etheses.dur.ac.uk/11838/.

38. Daniel Cash, *Regulation and the Credit Rating Agencies: Restraining Ancillary Services* (Routledge 2018).

39. SEBI, *Master Circular for ESG Rating Providers* (2023) https://www.sebi.gov .in/legal/master-circulars/jul-2023/master-circular-for-esg-rating-providers-erps -_73856.html.

40. FSA, *The Code of Conduct for ESG Evaluation and Data Providers* (2022) https://www.fsa.go.jp/news/r4/singi/20221215/02.pdf.

41. FCA, 'Code of Conduct for ESG data and ratings providers' (2022) https://www .fca.org.uk/news/news-stories/code-conduct-esg-data-and-ratings-providers.

42. HM Treasury, *Future Regulatory Regime for Environmental, Social, and Governance (ESG) Ratings Providers* (2023) https:// assets .publishing .service .gov .uk/ government/ uploads/ system/ uploads/ attachment _data/ file/ 1147458/ ESG_Ratings_Consultation_.pdf.

43. SEC, 'SEC Proposes Rules to Enhance and Standardise Climate-Related Disclosures for Investors' (2022) https://www.sec.gov/news/press-release/2022 -46.

44. SEC, *The Enhancement and Standardisation of Climate-Related Disclosures for Investors* (2022) https://www.sec.gov/rules/proposed/2022/33-11042.pdf.

45. Isla Binnie and Ross Kerber, 'DeSantis signs sweeping anti-ESG legislation in Florida' (2023) Reuters (May 3) https://www.reuters.com/business/sustainable-business/desantis-signs-sweeping-anti-esg-legislation-florida-2023-05-02/.
46. Robin Wigglesworth and Eric Platt, 'S&P Global's $44 bn deal shows data is the oil of the 21st century' (2020) Financial Times (Dec 1) https://www.ft.com/content/cd99579c-e01f-4a71-a124-e9c03598e5b9.
47. Dragon Y Tang, Jiali Yan, and Chelsea Y Yao, 'The Determinants of ESG Ratings: Rater Ownership Matters' (2022) SSRN (Jun 6) https://papers.ssrn.com/sol3/papers.cfm?abstract_id=3889395.

5. Systemic signalling: the application of signalling theory to the ESG rating space

1.   INTRODUCTION

The focus on the ESG rating space has been steadily increasing over the past few years. As academic research from a variety of disciplines ramped up, trade organisations began to focus more and more on the industry, its failings, and what the users – the investors – wanted from the space. On the back of such pressure, regulators have been brought into the equation, with regulators and legislators from around the world answering the call of IOSCO for, at least, a set of minimum standards to be applied in the fledgling industry. However, if one were to read all the criticisms and issues raised about the ESG rating space, one would quickly realise that there are voids in the narrative. Researchers who have adopted a pro-investor viewpoint have argued loudly that there are divergences within the industry, without explaining what should be done about it, and investor groups have surveyed members who have all stated that it is proving difficult to use ratings, but again do not offer concrete solutions for what should happen. One may believe, then, that the ESG rating industry is failing, without a plan on how to meet the demands of its environment, but this is not the case. Something is going unsaid by all these actors.

This book attempts to speak about that which is going unsaid. The book posits that the sole utility of a rating is to *signal*, and that if that sole utility is to be realised, a *natural oligopoly*, driven by investors, must come about. If this is the case, you can see why there is something going unsaid, because in the economic, political, and social climate we exist within, monopoly and oligopoly have negative connotations. Whole departments of government exist to prevent monopolies and oligopolies and, where they do exist, they are closely monitored. This book is not a champion of oligopoly, and nor am I as an author. In fact, in many areas of life, the concept would rightly be viewed as a negative. Yet, in the financial sector and with regards to the inter-relationships that dominate the capital markets, the informational flow that we have discussed and will further assess in this chapter is *fundamentally dependent* upon the concept of oligopoly. It may not be pleasant or comfortable to hear for economic purists, but the reality is the reality. There is a reason why there is so much focus being (consciously or unconsciously) mobilised to focus on related issues in the ESG rating space, and why in the credit rating space the agencies actually grew and became more dominant in the wake of the Global Financial Crisis (GFC) and all of the regulations and legislation that was passed, not the opposite. As the signallers for the system, they are intrinsic, integrated, influential, and, above all else, the core of the modern economic system the global society relies upon.

To explain this viewpoint, the chapter will first introduce the concept of *signalling theory*. It will do this first from a conceptual perspective, in analysing the founding thinkers and their development of the theory, and then by using the early application of the theory to examine whether there is any crossover into the rating spaces. Once that initial foray is completed, there will be a diversion into the concept of a *natural oligopoly*, as it is an important cornerstone to the viewpoint being advanced by this book. From there, the chapter will present an applied understanding of the two concepts to the world of ESG ratings, borrowing also from the world of credit ratings. The chapter will analyse each identified relationship in the informational flow so that we can see how each relationship is affected by the theory of signalling, but also how the concept of a natural oligopoly plays out for the parties in those relationships. After breaking down each relationship, it will be important to tie everything together because, after all, the financial system is a system comprising many parts.

The chapter will then return to the concept of liability that was explored earlier in the book. This is because there is a critical duality that currently exists in the ESG rating space that will be crucial to its future, and it is evident when we use the perspective of liability. By understanding what the ESG ratings may be used for with respect to liability, but then also how the ESG rating agencies themselves may be exposed to liability, we can potentially see the future direction of the nascent industry. Lest we forget, the word liability has not been referred to once in any of the regulatory or legislative initiatives that focused on the ESG rating space. This may be for good reason, because, as we know, the development of liability in the credit rating space has been fraught with difficulties, but the reality is that the question of liability *will* be applied to the ESG rating space at some point, and likely earlier than many think, given the ESG rating space is becoming more formalised by the second with all of the research, news, and regulatory focus being applied to it. Getting ahead of the curve by understanding some of the underlying issues that will potentially affect the space will be an important endeavour. Yet, before we get into the nuances of these issues, we must first equip ourselves with a solid theoretical base upon which we can apply the realities of the ESG rating space, and to do that we shall begin with the concept of signalling.

2. SIGNALLING THEORY

The conceptualisation of the theory of signalling is really simplistic at its core, perhaps indicating its almost universal coverage. Bird and Bird tell us that 'more broadly, signalling theory is concerned with how and why organisms exchange otherwise hidden information about each other or the world around them',[1] whilst Bolton and Dewatripont explain further that signalling is witnessed throughout nature, from the mating routines of peacocks to the intricacies of corporate finance and everything in between.[2] We have alluded to the concept throughout the book but, at its very core, the theory is the based on the fundamental concepts of communication, positioning, and perhaps more existentially, the concept of trust.

Wolf describes the development of the theory for us, telling us:

> Signaling theory emerged in the early 1970s, when George Akerlof, Michael Spence, and Joseph Stiglitz started to study the economy under conditions where information in interaction processes is asymmetric and not perfect, as thought for more than a century. This new perspective on information changed the paradigm of information economics and deeply affected the findings of the past. The scholars found evidence for four major recognitions: 'it is now recognised that information is imperfect, obtaining information can be costly, there are important asymmetries of information and the extent of information asymmetries is affected by actions of firms and individuals.' In 2001 they received the Nobel Prize for their analysis of markets with asymmetric information. Today, signalling theory is one of the most influencing and important information economics theories that is used in disciplines from management, marketing and human resources to psychology, sociology or anthropology.[3]

There were several founding thinkers in the field of signalling theory, though Akerlof and Spence stand out as early pioneers. In 1970, George Akerlof highlighted what he termed the 'lemons problem',[4] describing 'those situations in which buyers need to evaluate the quality of goods offered by sellers in a situation of information asymmetry. If buyers do not have enough information about the quality of goods sold, sellers of lower quality goods (lemons) can exploit the information asymmetry for themselves (moral hazard). In this situation, buyers could overestimate the price of lemons.'[5]

In 1973, Michael Spence published his seminal work *Job Market Signalling*,[6] which 'utilised the labour market to model the signalling function of education'. The brilliance of this conceptualisation described how 'potential employers lack information about the quality of job candidates. The candidates, therefore, obtain education to signal their quality and reduce information asymmetries.'[7]

This idea is directly useful for us, perhaps, as it infers that it is not exactly the quality of what is being sold, i.e., the job candidate, but crucially *how* they signal their quality that matters, i.e., the quality of their educational signal. To decompress further, a degree obtained from a universally respected university (say Oxford University, or Harvard University) conveys a seemingly 'stronger' message about the qualities of the candidate than a degree obtained from, say, a younger university, though, in both cases, the actual skillset of the candidate is not necessarily tested. This is because the receiver of the signal, the employer, either (a) recognises that prestigious schools have higher entry barriers, or (b) *believes* in the esteem of the university that is the vehicle for the signal, which can be a belief achieved in numerous ways. Essentially, the employer in this scenario is *trusting* that the graduate has obtained a variety of skills because, essentially, they *trust* in that educational institution to have both operated a higher-level screening process initially and then in a variety of ways imparted particular skillsets upon the job candidate in question. As you can see here, there is a lot going on that is unseen.

Within the theory itself, there are main antagonists, or parties. Wolf says that the theory operates with three elements: the signaller; the receiver; and the signal. On this understanding, Connelly et al. suggest that there is a procedure that is often followed, which consists of:

1. The signaller;
2. The signal is sent to the receiver;
3. The receiver observes and interprets the signal, and then decides whether to choose the signaller or not; and finally
4. That feedback is sent to the signaller, completing the loop.

However, there are issues with this understanding. The scholars follow this order up with the understanding that 'management researchers have found that signalling effectiveness is determined in part by the characteristics of the receiver. For example, the signalling process will not work if the receiver is not looking for the signal or does not know what to look for.'[8] There are also a host of other factors that may disrupt this order positioned by Connelly et al., like whether the signaller is in a position to be trusted to even send signals, whether the receiver has the organisational capacity to receive the signal, or whether they would even understand it if they received it. Also, what if the receiver is bound by competing factors whereby they may have to evidence how and why they are choosing particular signals over others?

You can see why here that the intricacies of life mean that theories can only ever take you so far. This is why, in relation directly to the capital markets but perhaps more broadly the financial realm, I have adapted Connelly's order to the following:

1. Signaller (person, product, or firm that has an underlying quality and needs to convince others of it);
2. The information on the underlying quality is sent to a perceptively independent third party;
3. The third party codifies this information and transforms it into an easy-to-understand signal, which is sent to receivers;
4. The receiver observes and interprets the signal from the third party and chooses to absorb it, or not;
5. Feedback is sent back to the initial signaller via the successful absorption of the signal (via investment, payment, or other completion of the loop).[9]

This evolved understanding is based upon the observation of Connelly et al. that it is the position and capability of the receiver that is critical.

This issue also relates to the concept of outsourcing. Say, for example, a firm wants to issue debt; it is very unlikely that they will care who invests in it and, in reality, it is in the firm's interest if many potential investors have the opportunity to invest as it will likely reduce the amount of interest they would have to pay on the issuance. To make that happen, the firm would have to evidence their creditworthiness in a way in which the entire market for investors could understand, at once, because otherwise, the costs associated with the action would be overly prohibitive. Also, why would the investors trust in the firm to evidence their creditworthiness when they have every reason other than reputational damage to inflate their actual creditworthiness? You can see here how credit rating agencies traditionally, and more recently ESG rating agencies when a firm is seeking to show their ESG credentials to the marketplace, exist. Spence, in discussing the works of Coase and Williamson, amongst others, states that 'generally, on the side of outsourcing is the likelihood that certain function can be performed better by specialists who have advantages of economies of focus and scale'.[10]

Yet, this concept of there being an order is a theoretical ideal, not reality. In reality, the order is often messy and infected by other issues, which all decrease the effectiveness of the overarching system. So, whilst it is true that 'a growing number of researchers and practitioners have identified the importance of intermediaries to mitigate risk, reduce information asymmetries and make the necessary link between the demand for and supply of investment capital',[11] its importance does not necessarily link to efficient and effective delivery. We will assess the different relationships within the demand for and supply of investment capital later in the chapter, but critical issues should now be familiar to us at this stage of the book, like when De Haan questions whether 'the results [of signalling theory] remain valid when noise is introduced into signalling technology'.[12]

The role of the third party, then, particularly in the financial arena, is crucial. This is for a variety of reasons. Bergh et al. discuss how third parties add benefit to the system by incurring the costs of absorbing the signal for the receiver and articulating it, or translating it, as appropriate, so that not only are the signallers reducing their costs via decreased duplication costings, the receivers are also having their costs reduced at the same time.[13] Pollack et al. attempt to evolve Burt's 1992 works – which suggested that there are structural holes within networks – by further suggesting that the existence of holes within networks provides ample room for third-party mediators to connect the informational flow between actors.[14] This, as a concept, makes sense when we understand that such 'holes' in networks exist because of base, elemental emotions and understandings like trust, and the lack of it. This is further enhanced as an idea when the scholars confirm, quite rightly, that not only are the holes in the networks rarely equivalent, but that it is also the case that, quite often, those 'holes' are exploited or strategically created so that associated industries can develop and take part in the network's system. Irrespective of this, whenever there are voids or holes that need to be bridged, having one's position mediated is of critical importance.[15]

The concept of signalling and the theory behind it is a wide and expansive one. However, to streamline our analysis and move towards the rating systems, it is worth considering *how* those signals are delivered in the capital markets, and *why*. Let us imagine that I as an investor want to invest $1 million, and I do not know where to start. I may not trust when a particular issuer says they are going to achieve x, y, or z in a particular timeframe, and all I am concerned with is simply (a) will I receive all of my investment back with the agreed-upon interest as my compensation/incentive for lending, and (b) will I receive it all back on time, as agreed? To understand those basic elements, and trust in the responses I receive, I would need a seemingly independent third party that could translate all of that for me in a way I can understand. In that regard, the credit rating agencies are perfect, especially with their easy-to-understand rating scale that is broadly the same across all agencies (note, this is why rating scales and the translation of them is such an issue in the ESG rating space). However, what if there are simply too many providers of those signals to me as an investor? It quickly becomes problematic and could disincentivise me to provide my resources for lending. To understand how this has been resolved, at least in the credit rating space, we need not look further than the concept of a *natural oligopoly*.

3.   NATURAL OLIGOPOLY

The study of duopoly and oligopoly also has clear origins, like that of signalling theory. Puu discusses how 'nobody would deny that Augustin Cournot in 1838 in his *Researches sur les Principes Mathematiques de la Theorie des Richesses* both formulated the problem, and presented a fairly extensive analysis of it. Further, it was one of the earliest economics treatises to be formulated as a mathematical model.'[16] Stroux explains that Stackelberg developed and evolved Cournot's understanding in that 'while in the Cournot model each firm takes the other's actions as given, in the Stackelberg model, one firm takes the other firm's reactions as a given. In his model he analyses whether it pays more for a firm to either be a follower or a leader in the setting of output.'[17] The core of the theoretical conceptualisation of duopoly and oligopoly is the interactivity between the duopolistic or oligopolistic players. Stroux continues by confirming:

> if one firm decides to be a follower and the other a leader, the outcome is called a 'Stackelberg equilibrium'. If each chooses to be a follower, and each firm expects the other firm to be a follower, the Cournot equilibrium will be the outcome. If both firms, however, choose to be a leader, the outcome is indeterminate; this situation is called 'Stackelberg warfare'.

Hall and Lieberman suggest that the concept of oligopoly 'presents the greatest challenge to economists' because whilst other market formats revolve around the concept of firms acting independently to focus solely on maximising profit, this does not neatly describe an oligopolist: 'the essence of oligopoly, remember, is *strategic interdependence*, wherein each form must anticipate the reactions of its rivals when making decisions. Thus, we cannot analyse one firm's decisions in isolation from other firms.'[18] The scholars then argue that this is why economists' tools have been adapted to deal with the realities of oligopolistic behaviours, so that theories such as game theory are now often utilised to understand and predict the behaviours of oligopolists.

Hall and Lieberman discuss later in their work that an indicator for different formats of market models can be seen in how the market participants advertise their services/products. They say that 'advertising is almost always found under monopolistic competition and very often in oligopoly. Why? All monopolistic competitors, and many oligopolists, produce differentiated products. In these types of markets, the firm gains customers by convincing them that its product is different and better in some way than that of its competitors' but, in relation to credit and ESG ratings, there are no such advertisements. There are reasons for this.

It could be because, as Hall and Lieberman discuss, a natural oligopoly is a market 'that tends naturally towards oligopoly because the minimum efficient scale of the typical firm is a large fraction of the market'. They also discuss that, in essence, the search for oligopolistic markets is really a search for barriers to entry, since that is what defines every oligopoly. They utilise the concept of economies of scale as one potential barrier, in that the minimum efficient scale for a typical firm in the market is a relatively large percentage of the market, resulting in lower costs per unit, which excludes smaller firms. This does not, necessarily, describe the rating marketplaces, as smaller entities do exist and perform functions. The next concept the scholars use is reputation as a barrier to entry, which very much affects the credit rating sector and is a growing factor in the ESG rating sector. The scholars talk about the high costs versus smaller revenues in the early battle to gain reputation in an oligopolistic marketplace that contains traditionally reputable firms as being the major prohibitor for entry, which makes sense. However, there are also strategic and legal barriers that the scholars identify, like when the oligopolistic leaders will lobby against proposals to increase competition for example, or when legal barriers exist like patent or copyright protections, or regulatory barriers like onerous registration procedures (think the NRSRO registration procedure that did not have a new registrant make it through in more than three decades).

The rating oligopolies, and I include ESG rating agencies in that definition for reasons which will become clear shortly, do have plenty of indicators of being established and potentially irreversible oligopolies. For example, Ellickson discusses how technological development in oligopolies is observed at the fringes and then consumed by the top of the oligopoly, which we see with the rate of M&A activity in the rating spaces, and also that oligopolists constantly have to dominate the space in order to survive, and we see that with the dominance of the Big Two in the credit rating space and then the concerted way that the Big Two have moved into the ESG rating space to join the very biggest players like MSCI.[19] However, the key to understand the rating sector's relationship to the concept of oligopoly is not to look into the theoretical constructs of the usual oligopoly, or even the usual natural oligopolies, but in that of the investor-driven oligopoly.

Schroeder, and Schroeter, have explored this concept the most and it is widely recognised at this point.[20] The justification for thinking that the credit rating market is an investor-driven oligopoly, at least, comes from the realisation that even after the incredibly poor performance of the rating agencies in the creation of the GFC – and the subsequent legislative and regulatory endeavours that followed which focused on reducing systemic reliance on ratings and increasing competition – the oligopolistic order was 'completely unaffected'.[21] As we preliminarily discussed earlier in the book, the sentiment is that:

> The evidence suggests that the decisive barrier to entry rather resides on the rating market's demand-side, namely the investors' preference for a market with only a few rating suppliers: Since a central reason for credit ratings' usefulness to investors is that they reduce complexity by distilling a wealth of market information into an easy-to-process rating symbol, this advantage would be lost again, had the investors to assimilate and process ratings from a large number of competing credit rating agencies. Financial markets frequented by investors with a limited capacity to assimilate and process information – the latter being a natural characteristic of real-world investors, although not reflected in the theoretical economic model of an efficient market – therefore always result in an investor-driven natural oligopoly of rating suppliers, making attempts to increase the number of relevant credit rating agencies futile.[22]

This is, at its core, the answer to all the prevailing questions relating to the credit rating sector.

When we add into the equation studies on third-party independence, the situation becomes clearer still. Leyens, in discussing the role of informational intermediaries, says:

> information intermediaries are needed only where the appropriate level of information to implement a transaction is not already available or cannot be properly processed by the parties. Intermediaries verify or evaluate existing information or substitute missing information. Intermediation hence fulfils its transaction-enabling function by adding to the information level available to a party. From the view of the acquirer of a product or service, the intermediated information needs to be more reliable, accurate or complete than the information the offeree voluntarily provides. An intermediary will only be made use of by the acquirer, however, if the additional information can be expected to be credible.[23]

Yet, what does this all mean for ESG rating agencies? Are the rules and lessons emanating from the credit rating space translatable?

4. THE RULES TO THE GAME IN THE ESG RATING SPACE

The simple answer to the question above is a resounding 'yes'. The lessons and rules from the credit rating experience are directly translatable, it is just that the environment around the ESG rating agencies is slightly different. To further understand this, this section will simply break down the realities of the relationships that make up the ESG rating space, from within this signalling/natural oligopoly perspective this chapter has built up. Yet, in reality, the same question that plagues the capital markets is now plaguing the ESG-related investment space: how can I trust somebody I do not know, and also 'show my workings'?

The relationship between the concept of credit ratings and ESG ratings should be obvious, but is worth articulating. The credit rating agencies exist to offer opinions on the underlying creditworthiness of an entity (issuer, or issuance), whereas ESG rating agencies exist to offer an opinion on the 'ESG-ness' of an entity (issuer, or issuance). That sounds simplistic because it is, but the complexity and varied subjectivity of ESG, sustainability, and non-financial information makes the role of the ESG rating agency that much harder. There are questions asked of the ESG rating agency and its ratings that are not asked of credit rating agencies, such as, against whose standard does x apply? Is that definition universally agreed? Also, the aspects ESG ratings consider are often understood against much longer time horizons, making them inherently more subjective and subject to change. The traditional informational infrastructure that accompanies financial information, like auditing and distinctive economic theories, is simply not present in the world of ESG, which does not help the ESG rating agency. Yet, what is required of them is a similar standard of *signal*, which is where the industry is experiencing all of its problems. To understand this further, let us break down the key relationships.

4.1 The Issuer–ESG Rating Agency Relationship in the World of ESG

The issuers in the sustainability-linked investment chain are in a particular bind. In the traditional investment dynamic, the rules to the game are well established; the information provided by issuers (financial statements) are audited by law, whilst it is the issuers who pay the credit rating agencies to produce a credit rating, which also allows the issuer direct access to the rating analysts. Conversely, in the ESG investment dynamic, those same issuers are issuing debt into a system that has no real defined parameters of engagement and, in opposition to a system that has agreed-upon definitions of financial materiality, many of the definitions in the ESG space are massively contested. Additionally, much of the data is not audited at all. Finally, because it is the investors who majoritively pay for the ESG ratings to be developed, the issuers do not have direct access to the ESG rating analysts. Rather, they are often given questionnaires to fill out, and that is it. Where conversations take place with analysts, they are scant, and even then the responses to the questionnaire may be misinterpreted, so the issuer has to commit resources to essentially maintaining the rating through the development processes, instead of the other way around.

It is questionable which of these issues is the most impactful, but the overall sentiment is that it all coalesces into a deeply inefficient process. If the aim is for the ESG rating agency to form an effective signal for the issuer (signaller), the process does not elicit that yet. For example, the issuer will field requests from multiple providers of ESG rating agencies, meaning that their resources are spread thinner, as opposed to engaging more significantly with a smaller number of analysts. Also, the regulations and codes we discussed in Chapter 4 are only now trying to enforce the process of there being designated people within the agencies who issuers will build a relationship with, which has certainly not been the case so far, further contributing to the inefficiency.

Also, whilst the intention of this book is not to be an advocate of the issuer-pays remuneration system, it does have distinct advantages over the investor-pays system, and the ESG rating sector is proving that point. The relationship that is built up by the issuer-pays model between the issuer and the agency means that aspects such as having efficient channels within which one can raise concerns or grievances makes the whole relationship that much more effective. It is not an accident that the codes of conduct and the regulations established or proposed all indicate that ESG rating agencies need to do more to allow issuers the space to complain or raise grievances, because it is a critical part of the rating process. Under the investor-pays model, it is that much harder to achieve because the relationship simply is not strong enough.

The issuers have one goal when entering the rating dynamic, and that is to have a signal generated without revealing sensitive information into the marketplace, or at least as little as possible. Under the current ESG system, that signal is massively noisy because there are so many ESG rating agencies vying for position, it is inherently inefficient because of duplication costs and poor relationships between issuer and agency, and ultimately it contributes to a depressed system, whereas a more efficient relationship could breed a fertile and growing marketplace.

4.2   The Investor–ESG Rating Agency Relationship in the World of ESG

With the dynamics of the ESG rating sector being different from that of the credit rating sector, in that it is often the investors who are paying for ratings, the reality is that the relationship between the investors and the agencies is much more complex. Whilst investors pay for the ratings, they do not pay to *generate* ratings, but merely to access the information on the issuers. This is a critical difference, because an investor may want to secure a small number of ratings, similar to what an investor might have to do in the credit rating sector (often at least two). However, the lack of standardisation is becoming the critical factor in the ESG rating space, and it is no surprise that whole research endeavours are being dedicated to understanding what is being called *aggregate confusion*. The lack of standardisation between ESG rating agencies means obtaining the ratings on an issuer from, say, two ESG rating agencies means very little and, in fact, could lead to more confusion because they could be and so often are wildly different. From an investor's perspective, this is not helpful.

It is worth asking *why* it is not helpful, though. A lot of the surveys reveal a key issue that many overlook: the large institutional investors, who make up the majority of 'investors' in the marketplace, often respond that they do not use ratings, credit or ESG, for their informational value.[24] In fact, research has been quite clear that the informational content of ratings is extremely low. The reality is, as we now know, that the main driver for incorporating the ratings into the investment process is directly related to the principal–agent relationship we uncovered earlier in the book. If an investment manager is having to keep a record of their investment decisions and potentially articulate them to their principals, having two ratings from ESG rating agencies that are wildly different does not help in the slightest; in fact, it could even raise concerns. If the aim is to signal to the principal, which I argue it is amongst other aims (like signalling to regulators), then wildly differing ratings on the same entity are the exact opposite of what is required.

Even if differing ratings were to be considered, which they are not, then at least the justification could be sought from understanding how those differing ratings were arrived at. However, with the ESG rating process being particularly opaque at the best of times, and with the rating scales between the agencies and what underpins them not being widely correlative, the problem for investors is further amplified. We can add to this – although it is likely not as big a concern as other issues – the understanding that ESG rating agencies do not tend to make clear whether they are operating on a single- or double-materiality basis, which could skew the results. However, as most ESG rating agencies operated on a single-materiality basis, those that require a double-materiality approach often know how to obtain it (through contracting for specialist investigations).

4.3   The Regulator–ESG Rating Agency Relationship in the World of ESG

Though the regulatory approach since the GFC has been to strategically remove the state from the rating dynamic, mostly by removing any references to the usage of ratings within regulations or statutes, the reality is that even if regulators wanted to mandate via ESG ratings, they would struggle. This is for all of the reasons stated above, ranging from a lack of standardisation and agreement in the space, to opaqueness and divergence of ratings. However, this still affects regulators, because even though they are unlikely to mandate the usage of ESG ratings in their systemic approaches, they still need to rely on them as a communicative tool between themselves as the regulated subjects.

Most attempts to reduce regulatory reliance went along the lines of stating that entities should instead use any and all methods of creditworthiness assessment, rather than just ratings. In the sustainability realm, the legal infra-structure has not developed enough to get to the point where regulators are mandating what forms of sustainability-ness assessments should be utilised, but the concept will likely be the same, that it is for the entity to decide (i.e., an investment manager can choose what they use). This fundamentally puts the onus back onto the marketplace and removes the state from blame whenever the next crisis occurs, but regulated entities still need to be able to *signal* to the regulators what they have chosen to use in order to demonstrate what level of risk they have exposed themselves to. This is particularly important when it comes to systemically important investment vehicles, like pension funds. However, if ESG ratings are not comparable, do not have similar rating scales, have opaque processes, and a host of other issues, the strength of that signal between regulators and regulated entities is massively weakened.

For the regulator, they are in a quandary. Apart from India, which has taken the step to even slightly interfere with the methodological processes of its ESG rating entities, every other regulator has made it abundantly clear that infring-ing on the creative processes of the ESG rating agencies is simply not accept-able, so as to preserve the critical appearance of independence. Nevertheless, the system clearly is not working and there is no suggestion that the base standards that have been called for will rectify the issues. Compelling ESG rating agencies to train their analysts, reveal their methodological processes, and build better relationships with issuers does nothing for the key issues of divergence. This is because there is only one solution that no regulator would ever champion: oligopoly.

Even when it comes to things like rating scales, which would make things a lot easier, the regulators cannot compel. Only business practice can lead to the convergence the marketplace is crying out for, and on that front the state must remain silent. Even though the remunerative model is different in the ESG rating sector than in the credit rating sector, the driving force is exactly the same: investors. Investors require clean and easy-to-understand signals that are comparable in order to release their funds and meet their obligations to themselves (agent to principal) and to regulators, especially when it comes to systemically important investors. In order to achieve that, the simplest and most effective way is to have far fewer players who would then go on to dominate the marketplace. The exact number is not really important, but the fewer the better is preferable whilst still retaining the appearance of choice. Unfortunately, for regulators, they cannot affect this trajectory and must sit by and watch until it all comes about. The main question then becomes whether the regulators and legislators will be ready and able to effectively regulate an ESG rating oligopoly, with the evidence from the credit rating sector suggesting that it is certainly not a forgone conclusion.

5.   THE CALL FOR OLIGOPOLY

Before concluding this chapter, I would like to take the opportunity to talk to you, as the reader, directly. This is important, because there may be sentiments that I have portrayed throughout which you may believe to be *my* views. However, this is not always the case. For example, I am no champion of an oligopoly and understand deeply the problems that come with oligopolies, especially when it is a natural investor-driven oligopoly like the credit rating oligopoly. The credit rating example is one that has caused distinct pain whilst producing nothing but pure profit, with the consequences of the transgressive behaviour of the leading oligopolists resulting directly, in my opinion, in the untold misery of generations. I am of the opinion and remind people constantly that without the active and conscious participation of the credit rating agencies in the lead-up to the GFC, it could not have existed. However, with all that being said, the reality is that the ESG space is currently suffering from a logjam. I often liken it to a reservoir full of investment and resources, but without the dam to harness its power. The marketplace is becoming extremely vocal as to what it needs and what it wants, but you have to listen closely to understand its real message. It is calling for *order* the likes of which only a concentrated and focused oligopoly can provide. It needs the signals required in order to allow information to move around the system, with rich resources following closely behind. The current ESG rating system cannot deliver that because it is too noisy, too fragmented, and simply not focused. Something has to give.

How that oligopolistic dominance will come about, I do not know. I would predict, if I had to, that the large credit rating agencies will take their place at the head of the oligopoly alongside the largest players like MSCI and Bloomberg. Some of the fringe players may remain, like CDP, which is only considered fringe to my mind because of what it offers, not its importance, and others like EcoVadis. But, for the most part, we will likely see fringe players swallowed up in strategic mergers to form the oligopolistic structure. It could even be the case that existing players are pushed out through sheer unattractiveness, because it should not go unmentioned that, interestingly, across almost every survey, Fitch's offering ranks last for usefulness and attractiveness; it is not outside the realm of reason that Fitch scales back and sells whatever business it has to the highest bidder (likely another rating agency).

If a new ESG rating oligopoly forms, there will be new questions to ask. The efficiency that the new oligopolistic structure would bring would likely result in a much greater flow of sustainability-linked investment, which would be celebrated. However, the transgressive behaviour that revealed itself within the credit rating oligopoly could easily be transplanted into the ESG rating space, especially if we see the development of exotic products to meet the investors' needs, complete with qualified buyers and difficult-to-understand underlying metrics. On top of that, I strongly predict that the European Commission's bold attempt to ban ancillary services in the ESG rating sector will not hold, or at least be circumvented, so that, in some fashion, they exist. This is because it is simply far too lucrative for the ESG rating space, especially as sustainability-linked investments could relatively explode if the oligopolistic structure I predict here takes hold. If so, the potential consequences for an ESG rating sector that can also offer ancillary/consultancy services could be significant, with economic rent-taking resulting in era-defining failures. Legislators and regulators would do well to proactively prepare for regulating such occurrences.

Oligopolies are not inherently bad, and quite often are *needed*. In the case of ESG and sustainable investment, it is certainly the case that oligopoly in the ESG rating sector would solve a lot of identified problems. Yet, whilst they should not be feared, they should definitely be a cause for concern and caution. Unfortunately, if my prediction is right and the dam begins to flow once the ESG rating problem is dealt with, the market will be in a euphoric state and in no mood to proactively regulate and heed warnings. Perhaps in that sense, then, the ESG and sustainability investment space will be a microcosm of the marketplace in general.

6. ESG RATING AGENCIES AND LIABILITY

It is interesting that none of the regulations being established or proposed, and obviously none of the codes of conduct, mentioned the word liability once. This perhaps makes perfect sense when we understand, as we do after analysing the issue in this book, that liability is a difficult concept to apply in the world of ratings. The reason as to why is directly found in this chapter, because if something is providing a critical service to the financial marketplace more generally, then applying liability to that entity is very difficult indeed. However, there is another issue that is raised when we consider the concept of liability and its connectedness to the ESG rating space.

The first issue is how the ESG ratings will be used. In Chapter 3 we saw how many agents, whether investment managers or corporate directors, have a multitude of duties that they are affected by. With those duties in mind, signalling to both one's principals but also regulators and/or relevant laws (via legal proceedings) is of critical importance to agents. The question then arises whether the current iteration of ESG ratings is strong enough to provide such service. One would argue that the answer is probably not. It is unlikely that an investment manager would feel comfortable utilising ESG ratings for their investment decisions when the prospect of being questioned against one's fiduciary duties exists down the line. The same applies to corporate directors who may want to signal to their principals that particular strategies are worth pursuing because the market may be moving this way or that, as evidenced by higher ESG ratings, to give just one arbitrary example. The sentiment here is that one cannot yet rely on the ESG ratings because of the issues cited earlier, like divergence and opaqueness, but this is amplified many times over when one's liability is connected to the decision.

An associated issue is with regards to the ESG rating agencies themselves. The question of how liability may apply to the agencies themselves has yet to be tackled in the literature, and it should be, because the very high bar that was inserted in the credit rating space may not necessarily apply in the ESG rating space. However, the more important the agencies become to the wider financial system, the more likely that bar will be raised higher and higher so as to protect ESG rating agencies against legal action. We have yet to see the conditions that were present in the credit rating sector, where agencies colluded with issuers against investors (qualified or not), but that is not to say that those instances cannot be created in the ESG rating space. Agencies are slowly beginning to pull away from the investor-pays model, and the more that issuers come to need the signals being developed, the more incentive there is for ESG rating agencies to charge issuers for their ratings. Arguments such as 'it would be better for relationship-building with issuers' will be forthcoming in order to justify the change, but the effect could be similar to that witnessed in the credit rating sector, which is concerning. How liability may be applied to ESG rating agencies, and under what conditions, is important to consider.

7.   CONCLUSION

This chapter sought to provide the theoretical lens which the book has been hinting at all along. The understanding of signalling theory and of the concept of a natural oligopoly is fundamental to the arguments in this book, which has aimed to provide an answer to the many questions plaguing both the ESG and credit rating industries. In the credit rating sector, the questions have revolved around just how the industry managed to survive what it did in the GFC (and not only survive, but indeed flourish!), whilst in the ESG rating sector, the questions all revolve around how to make it work properly for all concerned. This book has argued that it is only by understanding signalling theory and the concept of the natural oligopoly that these questions, and others, can be truly answered.

This is because, once we pull back and look at things in a more systematic manner, the fundamental role of the rater becomes clear. Their informational injection into the system, in terms of analysis and knowledge, is limited at best. Research and market participant surveys are quite clear on this front. However, they provide a theoretical and systemic resolution to a key problem: information asymmetry. Informational asymmetry is, in essence, a problem that *must* be resolved; there is no circumventing it, ignoring it, or manipulation of it. One either resolves it, or not. The concept of the rater is the private answer to that problem. This concept of private is also important, because the private nature of the environment that surrounds all of the players we have assessed in this chapter is, essentially, the parameters of the game. It defines what can happen, and what cannot. It is for this reason that there is often an unseen dynamic that exists in relation to independence, because the uninitiated would say, after reading about the credit rating agencies, for example, how can they be independent when they actively colluded with issuers against investors? How can investors trust credit rating agencies after what they did? The answer is that (a) they have to because nobody else can provide the signals the investors require, but also (b) it does not really matter if the trust is not really there, as long as it is *theoretically* there. As long as the agencies can theoretically be trusted to be impartial, which is revealed by the fact nobody interferes in their methodological processes, for example, then the *perceived independence* is left intact and that is all that is needed to technically allow the signals they create to be utilised by market players. If one were to suggest that it is all smoke and mirrors, they may not be too wrong.

NOTES

1.   Douglas W Bird and Rebecca Bliege Bird, 'Signalling Theory and Durable Symbolic Expression' in Bruno David and Ian J McNiven, *The Oxford Handbook of the Archaeology and Anthropology of Rock Art* (OUP 2019) 347.
2.   Patrick Bolton and Mathias Dewatripont, *Contract Theory* (MIT Press 2005) 126.
3.   Sandra Wolf, *Signaling Family Firm Identity: Family Firm Identification and its Effects on Job Seekers' Perceptions about a Potential Employer* (Springer 2017) 32.
4.   George A Akerlof, 'The Market for "Lemons": Quality Uncertainty and the Market Mechanism' (1970) 84 The Quarterly Journal of Economics 3 488–500.
5.   Sara Trucco, *Financial Accounting: Development Paths and Alignment to Management Accounting in the Italian Context* (Springer 2015) 26.
6.   Michael Spence, 'Job Market Signalling' (1973) 87 Quarterly Journal of Economics 355–74.
7.   Brian L Connelly, S. Trevis Certo, R. Duane Ireland, and Christopher R. Reutzel, 'Signaling Theory: A Review and Assessment' (2011) 37 Journal of Management 1 39–67, 42.
8.   ibid 54.

9.   Daniel Cash, *Sustainability Rating Agencies vs Credit Rating Agencies: The Battle to Serve the Mainstream Investor* (Palgrave Macmillan 2021) 99.
10.   Michael Spence, 'Signaling in Retrospect and the Informational Structure of Markets' (2002) 92 The American Economic Review 3 434–59, 455.
11.   Marguerite Mendell and Erica Barbosa, 'Impact Investing: A Preliminary Analysis of Emergent Primary and Secondary Exchange Platforms' (2012) 3 Journal of Sustainable Finance & Investment 2 111–123, 113.
12.   Thomas de Haan, Theo Offerman, and Randolph Sloof, 'Noisy Signaling: Theory and Experiment' (2011) 73 Games and Economic Behavior 2 402–428, 402.
13.   Donald D. Bergh, Brian L. Connelly, David J. Ketchen, and Lu M. Shannon, 'Signalling Theory and Equilibrium in Strategic Management Research: An Assessment and a Research Agenda' (2014) 51 Journal of Management Studies 8, 6.
14.   Timothy G. Pollack, Joseph F. Porac and James B. Wade, 'Constructing Deal Networks: Brokers as Network "Architects" in the US IPO Market and Other Examples' (2004) 29 Academy of Management Review 1 50–72, 50.
15.   Ranjay Gulati and Monica C. Higgins, 'Which ties matter when? The contingent effects of interorganizational partnerships on IPO success' (2003) 24 Strategic Management Journal 2 127–44, 130.
16.   Tonu Puu, 'A Century of Oligopoly Theory 1838–1941' in Tonu Puu and Irina Sushko, *Oligopoly Dynamics: Models and Tools* (Springer 2013) 1.
17.   Sigrid Stroux, *US and EC Oligopoly Control* (Kluwer 2004) 8.
18.   Robert E Hall and Marc Lieberman, *Economics: Principles and Applications* (Cengage 2007) 303.
19.   Paul B Ellickson, 'Supermarkets as a Natural Oligopoly' (2013) 51 Economic Inquiry 2 1142–54, 1149.
20.   OECD, *Bank Competition and Financial Stability* (OECD Publishing 2011) 25.
21.   Ulrich G Schroeter *Credit Ratings and Credit Rating Agencies* in Gerard Caprio (Ed) *Handbook of Key Global Financial Markets, Institutions, and Infrastructure* (Academic Press 2013) 387.
22.   ibid.
23.   Patrick C Leyens, 'Intermediary Independence: Auditors, Financial Analysts and Rating Agencies' (2011) 11 Journal of Corporate Law Studies 1 33–66, 36.
24.   For the discussion on this see Frank Partnoy, 'Rethinking Regulation of Credit Rating Agencies: An Institutional Investor Perspective' (2009) Council of Institutional Investors – https://www.sandiego.edu/law/documents/centers/ccsl/credit_rating_agencies.pdf.

6.   Conclusion to *ESG Rating Agencies and Financial Regulation*

So, how do you balance trust with responsibility? The book started by asking this question, and it seems fitting to finish with it as well. We saw that the question is perhaps the most integral question that applies to all of the capital market system, if not the entire economy. It applies to it all quite simply because the question captures innately humanistic concepts that cannot be escaped. Finding that balance is crucially important, of course, but *how* the financial system finds that balance was what was of concern for us in this book.

One of the most efficient ways to do it is via the injection of third parties. We saw how the needs of the private marketplace in the antebellum United States were answered in the form of the early mercantile agencies, which quickly grew into the credit rating sector we know today. Those same inefficiencies, based on informational asymmetry, that blighted the expansionist United States are, to a large extent, the same inefficiencies blighting the expansionist ESG movement today. The inability to trust another entity with their claims, whilst also balancing the intricate pressures that certain responsibilities provide, mean that, again, it looks like third parties could resolve the underlying issues. However, as we stand today, the third parties best positioned to do this are significantly underperforming.

We learned that despite all of the intent, it was the *form* that was causing issues. Too many offerings, complete with a lack of focus and collaboration to come to agreements on critical services, is currently preventing the act of investing in a more sustainable manner from really developing. Because of that, the ESG rating industry is coming in for incredible criticism, with the world's many regulators each taking turns to try to effect positive change. But, in this book, we learned that this approach can only take you so far. There is a model in a related industry that provides the answer that everybody is looking for; it is just that the answer is a particularly uncomfortable one.

Calling for oligopoly is something we will not see. The state cannot call for it, investors cannot call for it, and the ESG rating agencies themselves cannot be seen to be calling for it. It is the elephant in the room. However, it is there, and everybody knows it. The tone of the criticism and the research focused on the ESG rating space all reads like a manifesto calling for oligopoly, if one reads it correctly. 'We need less divergence!' and 'we should be able to compare between you all more!' may not call for oligopoly directly, but there is no other solution that creates what everybody is calling for. Oligopolies cannot maintain if there are too many members, so whilst all the many ESG rating agencies could start cooperating more, an open model without internal competition cannot be sustained. Again, something has to give.

One can be confident that it will give, however. The marketplace will get what it needs simply because it must. The incredible resources that are pent up in the system awaiting the right infrastructure within which it can all be deployed means that there is too much incentive not to have the marketplace's demands met. The regulatory endeavours that started with IOSCO were never designed to resolve the issues, because it is abundantly clear that regulation is not the answer here: this is a private problem that only has a private solution. The start of the regulatory endeavour was a warning sign to the marketplace to get things moving, because with formalisation comes expectation, and the ESG rating sector will now be expected to get its house in order. One can expect considerable action in the next few years as we begin to see an institutional restructuring to meet very clearly defined needs. Many things may change, but the needs of the marketplace will not. They need a signalling system capable to allowing for the movement of millions, billions, if not trillions of dollars, and they will get it, come what may.

Index